I Made That!

How to Make Money Making Personalized Stuff

Cindy Brown

TLM Publishing House
Ozark, Missouri
http://www.tlmpublishinghouse.com/

I Made That!
How to Make Money Making Personalized Stuff
by Cindy Brown

Published by:
TLM Publishing House
Post Office Box 123
Ozark, MO 65721
orders@tlmpublishinghouse.com
http://tlmpublishinghouse.com

I Made That! How to Make Money Making Personalized Stuff support website for question and answers can be located at http://press2success.com/imadethat/.

Copyright © 2004. All rights reserved. No part of this book may be reproduced or transmitted in any form or by any means, electronic or mechanical, including photocopying, recording or by any information storage and retrieval system without certified written permission from the author.

Trademarks: Author/Publisher make no claim of affiliation with or ownership of the Brand names mentioned in this publication.

Limits of Liability/Disclaimer of Warranty: The author(s) and publisher(s) of this book have given due diligence in compiling the information given. They believe all information to be accurate. They make no representation, claims or warranties as far as the completeness, accuracy, or merchantability.

All information is believed to be true and accurate. However, in any business, variables may affect any results. No implied guaranty of success is intended nor will any liability be accepted in any form.

Designed by Cindy Brown
Edited by Drew VanKrevelen
Photos by Courtney Ruby and Cindy Brown

Brown, Cindy
  I Made That! How to Make Money Making Personalized Stuff
  Includes bibliographical references and Index.
  ISBN 0-9748829-0-9
  Library of Congress Control Number: 2003099568

1. Small Business 2. Entrepreneurship 3. Crafts 4. Hobbies 5. Business Startup 6. Business Opportunities

Acknowledgements

Writing this book has been such an experience. A culmination of several years of studying, gaining experience, and then teaching what I had learned. Since beginning my business, and through writing this book, I would say I averaged about fourteen hours a day dedicating myself to the business, leaving only a few remaining hours a day to spend time with my children. All of this to *be* with my kids. Was it worth it? You betcha!

I want to thank my children, Courtney and Colton, for their almost-constant patience and support. They are why I worked so hard over the years, and they've been by my side through it all. They are truly my little miracles.

This book might not have come to fruition if not for the extraordinary help of my editor, Drew. His ideas, suggestions, and patience with me in making our first book was truly a Godsend.

Of course, if not for Don, I might not be in this business at all. He has been an enormous source of support since the day I found him on the Internet. He touches so many lives in this industry and asks for nothing in return. He is, without question, an answer to prayer for so many of us. To him and all of my friends who helped me through this growing process, I thank you from the bottom of my heart.

And last but not least, my dad. Without his patience and gentle guidance, I wouldn't have grown to believe that I could accomplish what I set out to achieve!

Table of Contents

Acknowledgments 3
Forward 7

A - The Plan & Set Up
A1 Greetings From the Author 9
A2 Get Your Head Straight 19
A3 Methods of Creating Business 23
A4 Setting Up Your Own Custom Heat Transfer Business . 32
A5 The Equipment – A Closer Look 35
A6 Money Matters 59

B - Tutorials & Training
B1 The Other Systems 66
B2 Dye Sublimation 71
B3 Thermal Vinyl 75
B4 Signs 77
B5 Tutorials 81
B6 Printers & Scanners 82
B7 Aligning the Transfer 100
B8 Transfers onto Whites 111
B9 Transfers onto Light Colors 118
B10 Transfers onto Dark Colors 123
B11 Transfers with Thermal Vinyl 127
B12 Transfers to Accessories 132
B13 Transfers onto Other Blanks 136
B14 Signs 139
B15 Refillers Guide 145

C - Reference & Extras

Q & A 157
Stay Up to Date on the Internet 167
Supplies/Vendor Directory 168
Resources 169
Glossary 175
Index 185
Chat With the Author 188

Forward

When I met Cindy she had just joined our transfer forum. She introduced herself on her first post as a "newbie." Well, she isn't a newbie anymore. She is an accomplished businesswoman and transfers expert.

I wish this book would have been around when I started. It would have saved me a lot of heartache, time, wasted shirts and money. I highly recommend it to anyone who is even thinking about going into digital transfers. It will save you a lot of trial and errors and a lot of wasted time.

Cindy is a stay-at-home mom/businesswoman with a daughter and young son. After a couple of months on the board, Cindy approached me and asked what I thought she could add to her business to help her make a living and still be at home to raise her children. After talking awhile about the pros and cons of digital heat transfers, she decided to go for it and go for it she did.

I have never seen anyone delve into something as fast and completely as she did. In a very short time, she was answering questions on about any subject that was asked. She impressed me so much that I asked her to become a co-owner of the Internet forum that I run. I have never seen anyone learn as fast as she did. Maybe that's because she was putting in from 12 to 16 hours a day at the time.

Cindy taught herself, asked questions, went to shows, called businesses and read whatever she could find on everything from inks, papers, printers, bulk systems, refilling carts and anything else she thought may help her cater to peoples needs. She is extremely knowledgeable about the entire world of digital transfers.

Forward

When she started, if someone asked her a question and she didn't have the answer, she would search it out, contact them and answer it for them. I have never known her to just leave someone hanging without an answer to their question.

I had the honor of meeting Cindy and her children when my wife and I went to Branson for a vacation. We got to spend quite a few hours with them over several different days and we just loved it. She is a very concerned and honest lady and an intelligent businesswoman.

Cindy considers her customers and board members more than just customers. She considers them friends and family and is very concerned with their progress and their success. I know of many times where she has done follow-ups with people to make sure things were going well. And I have read many posts on our Internet board praising her for her help and concern.

I've read posts where she was answering questions and giving help to new members as late as 2 to 3 a.m. She literally spends *many* hours a day on the computer, guiding people through their problems, answering questions and giving advice. I have never seen anyone as dedicated to helping other people as she is.

Cindy hasn't forgotten what it was like when she needed help and there was no book to learn from. Now, she is assembling and passing on what she has learned from her years of experience and study. I think this book will be a great source of information and support for you and I wholeheartedly recommend it!

Don Ford
Ford's Screen Printing
Heat_Transfers_For_Desktop_Printers@yahoogroups.com

Greetings From the Author

A little history, some rambling, and hopefully a lesson learned to share with you...

A long, long time ago, in a place not so far from here, I began my working life. I was fourteen years old, and was as nervous as could be to be starting my first job! I was one of those little girls who sell sodas and popcorn at the local amusement park. It was a dream come true for me.

Thus began a life of working for someone else. It was a blast. There were parties on the weekends. There were paychecks every two weeks. Life was so good... and fun!

By the time I reached eighteen years old, working a job wasn't fun anymore. (Big surprise, huh?).

My situation is probably quite different from most others in that I graduated early from high school to get married. No, I wasn't pregnant, but I just didn't know what to do with my future... so I thought getting married was the way to spend the rest of my life.

I thought I could be a house wife and cook and clean all day and life would be fun and exciting again (like it was when my first job was so exciting).

Imagine my surprise when doing dishes and cooking my specialty dinner of macaroni and cheese and fried potatoes became boring. What ever was I to do for fun and excitement then?

I know you're thinking to yourself, "What in the world is this crazy woman doing? She's writing a book about how

A1 » Greetings From the Author

to make money making personalized 'stuff', but all I'm reading is how stupid she was as a youngster." I promise the point is coming shortly.

So, here I am, married. What's next? Oh! Have a baby! So I did. Having my first child was the most amazing thing to ever happen to me. Somehow, I suppose it was one of those maternal things you hear about; something suddenly changed in me.

What was exciting before really wasn't all that much of a thrill any longer. What made me happy was being with my little girl.

The only real problem I seemed to have was that we weren't quite making the bills each month with me as a housewife. My husband told me that I needed to find a job.

Was he insane? Find a JOB? Leave my child every day? Not a chance! Then it occurred to me; I could open a craft store. I had done several craft shows over the past few years and, while I didn't make a lot of money, it was something to add to the kitty.

I talked it over with my husband and he agreed. I drove up and down the streets of our town, found a nice, cheap retail location and within the week I had opened my store!

Yee-haw! At the age of 20, I was a business owner. Hooray for me! Each day I would make a few more crafts to add to the empty store. Each week, I would have another bill for supplies. Heck, every now and then a customer actually came into the store.

You guessed it. Within a couple of months, instead of

generating income to help my family, my business had drained our finances even further. Thus ended my first store and the thought that I would ever be a business person.

We decided we would consolidate bills rather than getting me a job away from my daughter. Then it happened. My husband decided that since we really weren't happy with each other, and 'before we're too old to find other people,' that we should call it quits.

My world went upside down. I went back to my home town, ended up having to leave my daughter with a sitter morning to night while I worked two part time jobs and one full time job (back at the local amusement park no less, which somehow had lost all it's allure now).

I did what I had to do but swore to myself, that while my daughter spent days with someone else for the time being, it wasn't going to be like this for much longer.

About six months later, I admitted defeat and moved back in with my family. Yes, I was one of those who couldn't wait to leave home only to find that home is sometimes the best and safest place to be.

Instead of working three jobs, I worked one full time job. When I got myself back on my feet, I got my own place again and added another job... this time though, I was babysitting in the daytime and working at a pizza place in the evenings.

During these years, I tried everything to find some sense of fulfillment and manage to pay the bills at the same time. I remembered how happy I had been when I'd had my craft store and was able to have my daughter with me all the time. But of course, my lack of any real matu-

A1 » Greetings From the Author

rity (still only about 22) kept me from being able to really think things through and figure out a way to make a living, keep my daughter with me, and still be happy.

I tried MLMs (multi-level marketing companies), direct sales, cosmetics, every darn thing you could probably think of. If it was free or cheap to try, I did it. I bought into the hype of making tons of money and since my goal was always to be with my daughter, without an outside job, I gave them all a go. And then of course, gave them the heave ho. Many of the things I tried brought some limited success, but without the proper motivation, dedication and just plain logic... none were true successes.

I found real estate to be a pretty satisfying career change. While it was typically feast or famine, it seemed to fit me well. My love for teaching and helping others was fed. My need to feel like I was needed was met. And most of the time I was able to be with my daughter.

Upon remarrying many years later, becoming pregnant with my son, and seeing him in my arms that first few minutes of life (my children are thirteen years apart, by the way), I remember thinking, "I am so blessed. I get to do it all over again!"

I've told this story to several people in the business already but I really love it so I hope it's ok to share it with you now too.

About a week after the birth of my son, I received a customer referral from the real estate office. The couple was looking for a home in our area. They wanted to spend about $275-$350 thousand.

Remember now, I typically spent my time with first-time home buyers, teaching, helping, holding their hands through their first home purchase. Most people buying first homes aren't in this price range.

I knew our financial situation wasn't stable enough after taking so much time off with the bed rest of a fairly risky pregnancy. I knew I had to take this client. If I could sell them a house they liked, I could make my house payments and, in fact, probably all of our household bills for a year or more.

I put on my suit (which was in itself probably another story... squeezing into a size 10 suit with my 6- to 7-day post-partum body, but I'll spare you that one). I was dressed, had made the appointment, and I was ready to leave.

I went to kiss my little man goodbye; he was so precious. What a little miracle I'd been given. I would do anything for him and right then it was time to show him... by going to work.

I turned to leave but, by the time I reached the door, I was a blubbering mess of hormones. I couldn't make myself walk out the door. I had waited thirteen years to have another child and leaving him for any reason so soon after he was born just felt so totally wrong.

My husband realized a couple of things right then. First, if we were going to make this commission, he had to get me out the door. Second, he realized just how much love a mother can have for their child. Without thinking another second, he put on a nice shirt, told me to wipe my eyes, and out the door we went, my son, my husband and myself.

The clients thought it was adorable when I told them the story. We showed them the most beautiful homes I had

A1 » Greetings From the Author

ever seen in my life and, between each showing, our clients would coo happily at my little guy.

As it turns out, they bought a house in a town about an hour out of my area so I didn't get the sale but that experience showed me and my husband something; regardless of anything else, I needed to be with my kids or I would be miserable.

I'll skip the entire life story and summarize by saying this: I knew I enjoyed working for myself; I knew my kids were my main motivation to becoming financially secure; I knew that money struggles could happen more than once in a lifetime; and I needed to make sure that it wouldn't happen to me ever again.

Suddenly I found focus. I found that in order to be with my kids, I had to work my rear end off. Nothing tangible in life is free. It was time to roll up my sleeves. It was time to look further than a week into the future for a change. It was time to find a way to generate an income that would feed all of my needs, physical and emotional.

Now, I'm finally getting to the point. Being a new mommy, I wanted to do cutesy crafty things for my baby. I bought an inexpensive embroidery machine. I realized quickly however that while my son had the cutest darn clothes in town, I couldn't find a way to sell them because the local discount store was already selling everything I could but at half the price.

I questioned myself again then. I had thought it through, right? I saw embroidery everywhere in stores so the demand must be huge. It's creative, fun and just tickles me to watch the needle make an airplane on a pair of little jammies.

Whoa, wait a minute... Was I really thinking? Or was I just letting my heart make my business decisions? Did I investigate the competition before spending my money? No, not really.

Had I checked to see if it was legal to sell those cute Big Bird® designs from the cards that worked with my machine? Nope. I found out after I bought them that I could use them on my son's shirts but not on something that would be sold for profit.

Good grief! You try to try to get ahead and it seems that, no matter what you do, something always stands in your way.

Now it was time to really think, to take my emotions out of the picture entirely. For me, this isn't very easy to do. But it was clear that if I were going to be successful enough to build a business that could keep me home with my kids, it was time to think with my brain, not with my heart.

I investigated the local competition in the embroidery industry and there seemed to be a lot more competition than I had hoped to find. But, in visiting some of these businesses, I saw some cute little photo mugs and t-shirts with photos on them. "Hmm," I thought to myself, "I wonder if those are popular?"

Now, thinking more logically, I got on the computer and checked out an auction site. I briefly investigated what I would need to start a business selling personalized coffee mugs. When I spoke with one of the sellers, I was told I would need one of their used printers that had been recycled for use in this new business. After I scraped together the money for this special type of printer, I

A1 » Greetings From the Author

found out that I would also need a special mug press. "Why didn't he tell me that in the first place?" I wondered.

The mug press was even more expensive than the used dye sublimation printer. I swallowed hard and decided that nothing worthwhile was going to come free so I ordered a mug press from this person as well.

Then I found out that I had to buy special papers and special mugs..."Special MUGS? Is this guy for real or is he trying to charge me for mugs that I could get at a local store, for crying out loud?" (In case you haven't heard yet, yes, it does require a specially coated mug, but of course I didn't know that at the time).

By the time I was done "shopping," my $295 business start-up expenses had grown to something around $1,300.

Do you remember when I said that I briefly investigated what I would need? Had I investigated a little more fully, I would have known ahead of time that one printer without the other items wouldn't do me much good. Had I investigated even further, and spoken to more than one vendor, I would have known that my first $1,300 setup was going to be virtually worthless for what I really wanted to do.

Had I investigated better in the beginning, I might not have purchased a flat heat press that was smaller than I really needed for t-shirts and other items. So... I ended up selling my brand new heat press on eBay (at a loss, of course) and buying a considerably larger press.

I also needed to sell my nearly new mug press and ended up using the case of special mugs as dust collectors since selling them on eBay would have meant high shipping charges and the risk that they would break before they even made it to the buyer.

I even had to send the used printer back to the initial vendor and buy a new dye sublimation printer from one of the 'big guy' vendors in the industry. After all that, I realized that even with the new printer I still couldn't get the results I wanted.

It was only by repeated trial and error that I finally figured out how to succeed, that and my sheer determination not to give up this one last time.

I made the exchanges, kept reevaluating and adding different items, until at last I found a system that I was not only satisfied with but happy with. Finally, I was on my way!

Now, my question to you is this: do you want to fumble around like I did for several months and possibly several thousand dollars? Or would you like to find a way to bypass most of that mess? If so, keep reading and we'll see if we can't help you get up and running with minimal expense and a whole lot less trial and error!

If this story scares you away from the industry completely, that's okay too. I would rather scare you off now than know that you spent your hard-earned money and a lot of your time and trouble on something that you didn't have the determination to follow through on.

If my story didn't scare you but made you realize that you need to become a wise consumer, then I've done what I set out to do.

I believe that you can and will be a success in this

A1 » Greetings From the Author

industry. Personalized items are becoming very popular. If you're old enough, you might remember a time in the 70's and 80's when everyone had monogramming machines that were able to put big initials on their shirts. Those days seem to be coming back.

Now, instead of big cheesy monograms, the personalized products industry is growing like wildfire with photo products, school sports apparel, and small businesses who can't afford to screen print in large quantities.

There is, without question, a market for personalized products. If you set yourself up with a quality system that can make professional products, if you're dedicated to working your way to success, and if you find that you enjoy creating items like these as much as I do, then I think it's time to get started!

Get Your Head On Straight!

So you want to start your own business, huh? I'm sure you've heard the statistics so I won't elaborate on them now but a lot of businesses fail in their first year. What does that mean to you? You won't be one of the failed businesses, right? Or will you?

There are so many reasons why a new business might fail. One thing to remember, at least in my opinion, is that you will only fail if you allow yourself to fail.

As with many (if not all) business owners who are just getting started, if you educate yourself about your new business venture before (or at least at the beginning of) getting yourself set up, I believe you'll find becoming successful can be more of a reality than a dream.

A Business Plan

This is where having a business plan comes in. You can find a ton of books and Internet resources for how to create your business plan, and that's a little out of my area of expertise, but I can tell you that a solid business plan often equates to a solid business.[1]

The essence of a business plan is to help you to think rationally. I call this the 'Get Your Head On Straight' plan. You will find many examples as you investigate that are as many as fifty pages in length. Do not let this intimidate or deter you from your own goal of creating your business plan.

You don't need perfection. You don't need exact details. What you do need is to put onto paper, maybe in only a few pages, what you plan to do, how you plan to do it,

A2 » Get Your Head On Straight

why you feel your plan will be successful, what you will need, and any other pertinent information. An example outline could be as follows.

Executive Summary
   Highlights
      Objectives
      Mission
      Keys to Success
      Possible Roadblocks
Business Summary
   Products
Market Analysis
Strategy and Implementation
Management Summary
   Financial Plan

I have known some people who scribbled their business plan on a napkin and became very successful. That's completely acceptable if it works for you. If it will help you (or especially if you plan to try to obtain any sort of financing for your business), you will need to create a more professional format for your plan.

It's important to remember that one single thing does not make your business successful; one thing can, however, cause the ruin of your business. This is especially true if the one single thing is your failure to plan and think your business through.

If you have already purchased your equipment before doing the proper research and testing, it's still not too late to begin planning your success instead of simply 'thinking' about it. Hopefully, the worst case scenario would be that you made a purchase or two that wasn't really what you needed (I know I did). If that's the case, you can sell the item, use it as a backup, or donate it to a charity. If you made all the right purchases, you're that much ahead of the game. Congratulations; that kind of success is rare!

When you are preparing yourself mentally for your new business, think of the Golden Rule. With each choice you make when you determine your policies, ask yourself this question, "If I were a customer of my business, how would I want things to be done?"

Now, typically taking this mindset will automatically bring your new business a degree of success simply because when you are treat your customers well, they will tell their friends and associates about you. On the flip side, if you are thinking only of yourself and not your customers, you may begin to make decisions that will seem unfair to your customers. Once again, they will tell their friends and associates. This time, however, their comments will be negative and your business will suffer.

Do you remember those days when the old saying "the customer is always right" was used in almost every business? I don't know what changed (and that's another book entirely), but if we take the attitude that we are here to serve our customers until they are not only satisfied but thrilled with our service, we have done our jobs and earned our pay.

I completely believe that if you work hard to do what's best for your customers, they will be happy to spend their hard-earned money on your products. In fact, if you are consistently fair and helpful, your clients will become your loyal customers and will even go out of their way to recommend you to their friends.

A2 » Get Your Head On Straight

If you charge a reasonable price, offer options and timely support for your products, and show your customers that you genuinely care about their satisfaction, you really should be a shoe-in for success. If you don't have a genuine concern for your customers and their satisfaction, you might want to rethink whether you should be going into business at all. Enough said; let's get started!

---

[1] If you need further assistance, please visit the Resources section for an assortment of URLs and book titles to help you set up your business plan.

Methods of Creating Business

Start Planning

Who will you sell to? What will you sell? What makes you think you've got what it takes to start a business? Are you an artist? Do you have access to customers who have a need for these products? What makes you think you will be one of the successful ones?

Do some of these questions seem harsh? If so, stop and ask yourself why they seem harsh. Asking yourself questions now can save you hundreds of dollars and/or many hours of wasted energy.

The most important thing, in my opinion, isn't to know the answers to these questions, but to understand why you need to ask them of yourself. When you can begin to answer them, you're on your way to creating a solid foundation for your business.

You can use a separate piece of paper or write your answers right in the book but try now to answer the questions on the following page as best you can. Then, right before you plan to open for business, ask yourself these same questions again. Have your answers changed? Have you gained a better understanding of your market and the product line you plan to sell? Hopefully, the answer is "Yes!" If so, congratulations!

A3 » **Methods of Creating Business**

Questions to Consider

Who will you sell to?

What will you sell?

What makes you think you can start a business?

Are you an artist?

Do you have access to customers who have a need for these products?

What makes you think you will be one of the successful ones?

Marketing Basics

Find a Niche

An excellent way to develop a source of customers and products at the same time is to find or create a niche. There are so many possibilities that there are truly too many to mention here.

Take notes as we make some basic suggestions. Think of your own situation. Think of who you know, what you like, what you can do or what you have access to that can help you pinpoint your own niche.

Think of it this way: restaurants are very successful. That being the case, why do so many restaurants fail?

The restaurant concept isn't what failed. I eat out almost every day so I know that there are many successful eateries out there, many making quite a bit of profit. Sometimes the restaurants that fail do so because they don't offer a desired food to the local customers in that local.

When a restaurant starts out as a full service, fine dining establishment and serves steaks and seafood, the owner invests a lot of money in equipment, furniture, décor, etc. If, within six months, they realize that they can't succeed at that time in that place, what will they do? More than likely, they will sell what they can and go back to working for someone else or they may possibly reevaluate their situation and change their menu or move what they have to a new location.

When you determine your initial product line (what you will sell) and your market (who you will sell it to), you

A3 » Methods of Creating Business

might get lucky the first time and your new business might be a roaring wildfire of success.

If, however, you find that you are struggling to make ends meet, aren't getting enough jobs, or just can't seem to quite get your business off the ground, it's time to rethink. You should **reevaluate often!** There should be a reevaluation approximately once a month. I say this mostly because it is entirely possible that when you started your business, you did so based mainly on emotion (like someone I know well).

Do as I say, not as I did!

I have always loved Victorian things. All things "frilly" are right up my alley. When I started my business doing embroidery, my eyes caught every rose, Victorian hat, and items of this nature. I tried to create artwork that suited my taste. Do you know what happened? I collected a lot of cool "frilly" things and sold a whole lot of nothing. It was time to reevaluate!

What I am saying is that as you plan your product line, make sure that you think not only about what you like or dislike, but also what the market is currently. If western decor is all the rage in your area; don't make Victorian items. At least not unless you find your own little niche in spite of the popular trends.

You will find a similar experience is possible when it comes to purchasing equipment. If you start buying before you've investigated what you'll actually need, you can end up spending too much on equipment that you might have been better off without. This is unfortunate. However, it is not uncommon. It's not the end of the world if it happens. You're certainly not alone. But, if you can, make sure that you do your homework before you hand over your credit card numbers.

That said, it's also important that you keep your expectations realistic. You are not very likely to create a top-quality, commercial product on an investment of $500. I'm not saying you can't start with as little as $500, but you will need to realize that you will have a small press, a lower end printer, and so forth.

One of the most important things in business is making sure that you produce a quality product. If your product is not professional quality, you will not be able keep your customers. In fact, you'll probably be inviting trouble. People expect quality when they hand over their hard-earned money. Continued customer loyalty and repeat business along with referrals are what will keep you in business.

Who will buy your products?

Don't analyze yet; just brainstorm. Ask a friend or family member to bounce ideas around with you. Your goal is to come up with at least 10-20 possibilities for each of the areas below. Don't worry if you can't think of that many — you can start with a few ideas and add to them as you go along. Obviously, the more ideas you can come up with now, the easier it will be to find a few that will be successful for you.

Write down some ideas for products that you think will work for you. Then, come back to review these sheets right before opening for business. You might add some of these products later or, if your first ideas aren't as successful as you'd like, you've got some other possibilities to work into your product mix.

A3 » Methods of Creating Business

After completing the brainstorming stage, try to come up with a list of pros and cons for several of the products that you believe you would both enjoy and be able to profit from. Be sure to save this initial list. Come back to it often. Look for other possibilities and see if you can add new ideas to the list.

You want to be able to determine your own pathway but it isn't necessarily going to be the first one you choose.

Jot down a list of products that you think you'd like as well as items that don't necessarily appeal to you but you believe might be popular with your customers.

1. **Collectors:** Things that have a common theme such as panda bears, hats, landscape photos or paintings, clever or insightful sayings, etc.

2. **Clubs or affiliations (direct sales):** School organizations, team sports, commercial work such as small business t-shirt uniforms, church groups, motorcycle groups.

3. **Fundraisers (indirect sales):** Schools, church groups, motorcycle groups, etc.

4. **Flea markets**: Regular weekly locations, or traveling flea markets. There are publications[1] that track these, give demographics information and booth/space prices. Make sure that your products are suited for flea markets if this is going to be one of your methods of selling.

5. **Shows:** Shows can include craft shows or other selling opportunities. Mall booths or kiosks, traveling shows, etc. Again, these are typically found by word of mouth and through niche publications. Make sure that if

you want to exhibit in a craft show that your products are considered crafts. Take a look at the magazine section of a large bookstore for ideas of the many types of popular crafts that people might be interested in.

6. **Internet:** Without question, this is an important method of selling and a way to reach a wide range of potential customers. Be aware that the Internet is loaded with plenty of competition as well. I typically would not recommend that you count solely on the Internet to generate your sales.

If you are doing this as a hobby, it might work well for you. However, getting out there and wearing your product or otherwise displaying it for potential customers to see will greatly increase the chances of a purchase.

I strongly recommend adding a Web site as an additional method of generating sales but probably not as the only method. This is not something you have to do right away either.

7. **Cooperative ventures:** Is there another person or business that might work well in a joint venture with your business? Can they draw while you do the accounting and marketing, etc.? If so, this can be advantageous for both of you. Twice (or more) the work can add up to twice (or more) the sales.

Remember however, when starting a project with someone else, that many partnerships fail. Often, this is due to partners not fully discussing their individual roles, rights and obligations or maybe they discussed them but one or both parties didn't fulfill their part of the bargain.

My thought on this is that you only partner with someone you are reasonably sure you can trust. Think of

A3 » Methods of Creating Business

this... if your business explodes and you become very busy, will you be able trust that your partner will not try to take advantage of the situation. Do you trust them not to take or hide sales/income from you? You should be very careful who you partner with but a good partnership could also blossom into an excellent business.

8. **Retail location**: This is not a method I would recommend for an initial start-up without first doing some additional planning and budgeting. Often, having a retail location can burden you with the obligation of keeping regular office hours and the obvious additional financial obligations such as rent, utilities, insurance, etc.

You're probably best off starting your business out of your basement, office, or garage. Then, if and when sales start to take off, you can look into the possibility of opening a storefront.

If you have done your homework and are able to produce enough products to pay your bills and still generate enough sales to make it worthwhile, the properly placed retail location can sometimes make you an almost instant success.

Just remember, there are a lot of additional expenses involved in opening a "bricks and mortar" store. Plan ahead to be sure you can meet these obligations before committing yourself to anything long term.

9. **Home parties:** This method isn't used very often with small or beginning businesses, but if you model your parties after one of the highly successful companies that are already out there doing this type of marketing, I think you might be happily surprised.

There are ways to avoid the risks of retail, at least initially. You might want to have small booklets (or CD ROM discs) produced that show your product line and price list. Using the same concept as some of the 'big guys' (like the home décor, cosmetics, and kitchen accessories companies), your business could offer free items or highly discounted items to a party host/hostess for generating pre-set levels of sales for you. This could be a win/win situation for you and the person who hosts your party.

You might even want to give out free products or samples at the party to generate sales. This method can be and, in my opinion, should be used along with other methods (for instance, a home party for frog collectors, or a home party for the soccer club).

10. **Miscellaneous:** This list is only meant to help get you started. There are an infinite number of possibilities for marketing your new products. Jot down some of your own ideas as well. Highlight ideas that you especially like rather than crossing out those that don't sound as promising to you at first. Later, the ideas that you didn't think you liked may end up being the ones that make your business successful. Keep your mind and your options open!

---

[1] In the rear of the book I have assembled some outside resources for you to further investigate methods that you may want to consider for creating business. You can find them in the "Resources" chapter.

Of course, if you would like to find even more resources you can also use an Internet search engine. The Internet can be an abundant source of information once you know what to look for.

Setting Up Your Own Custom Heat Transfer Business

Much like making a yummy bread or cookie recipe, there is a recipe of sorts that you will need in order to create personalized products with custom transfers. Here, we will go over the basics and some of the specifics as well.

There are many variables as far as brands, types, etc. You should consider this book as a starting point for determining which items you will purchase for your initial setup. Your own budget and equipment needs should be considered for your specific business.

> 1) Computer
> 2) Software
> 3) Heat Press
> 4) Printer
> 5) Inks
> 6) Papers

Quick Summary

1) **Computer** - This one is probably the simplest of the required items. Many families have a computer already and as long as your computer can handle a basic to sophisticated graphics program, you should be fine.

With modern technology, you might even be able to get started without a computer if you purchase a special printer that will print directly from a media card. This can produce a very basic photo transfer to get you started.

2) **Software** - There are a lot of different graphics programs available but you can start with something as basic as a freebie program that came with your printer or scanner or you can opt for one of the more professional drawing or painting programs such as Corel Draw® or Adobe PhotoShop®.

There are even some programs available that provide t-shirt, mousepad, or puzzle templates to help you get started. Be careful with these "canned" designs however since to generate an income from their artwork might be an infringement on the copyright.

3) **Heat Press** - Some people ask me, "Can I use a home iron instead of a heat press?" The answer to that is difficult. Yes, you probably can, but... you will likely experience inferior quality, poor washability, reduced longevity, and much more frequently botched jobs. I strongly recommend against using a home iron for professional use.

If you want to make a few shirts for your family reunion, a home iron might do the trick. However, if you intend to generate an income by selling shirts and other items for profit, you will be expected to provide a professional quality product that stands up to repeated washing. I strongly advise that you start off with the proper equipment so that you don't risk tarnishing your reputation and ruining your business before you even get started.

4) **Printer** - This will likely be your most important single purchase. While many inkjet printers aren't too expensive, getting a top quality compatible printer for the job is imperative. Most of the best custom digital transfer creators use Epson® brand printers.

A4 » Setting Up Your Own Business

Be forewarned, though, not all Epson® printers are compatible so be sure to research the full system setup prior to buying a printer. (For more details please see the Supplies Directory in the back of the book.)

5) **Inks** - While many home users or hobbyists find that using the OEM inks that come with a printer are sufficient, most professionals who make custom commercial transfer products insist on using a quality pigmented ink set. There are several available through Internet supply houses. (Again, you can get more information in the Supplies Directory in the back of the book.)

6) **Papers** - A visit to a local office supply store will likely show you what type of paper many home or hobby users might find to print their transfers. Most of these are not of an adequate quality (in my opinion) to use for a professional product although they may be fine for low volume, short-term use, like for a family reunion or a gift/gag shirt. You can find commercial quality transfer paper easily on the Internet at prices that are likely much lower than the papers at the office supply stores.

We will cover these items in depth in the next chapter. If you are comfortable searching online, please reference the "Supplies Directory," "Resources," and "Stay Up To Date" sections at the end of the book.

You will also be able to get answers to your questions online through our Internet forum at:

http://press2success.com/imadethat/

Please feel free to use the forum as often as you like to find additional resources, suppliers and equipment information and updates.

The Equipment — A Closer Look

Computer

I'm going to assume that you have a basic working knowledge of computers. For the purposes of this business, you will not need to know much more than how to turn the computer on and run the software program of your choice.

Software

The software program (application) that you choose to use for your personalized product business (or hobby) can truly be as simple as a word processing application that can accommodate photos (and graphics) as well as text. If you want to create more sophisticated designs, you should look into getting a real desktop publishing and/or graphics application that could run as high as several hundred dollars.

There's no question that you'll have more flexibility and will be able to produce more sophisticated graphics with a professional program. With this in mind, I recommend that you purchase and learn (if you haven't already) a professional application such as Corel Draw, Adobe Illustrator, Adobe Photoshop and/or Macromedia Freehand.

There are several good graphics programs to choose from but, as I am most familiar with Corel Draw, that's is the one I'll be using for my examples. That doesn't mean that it's the only one that will do a super job though. There are several great programs out there.

A5 » The Equipment – A Closer Look

You could also ask around on Internet user groups as well as asking friends and family who have graphics programs to see which they recommend. Taking into consideration your budget and the particular needs of your business is very important. If you can't afford a program like Corel Draw from the start, you can certainly start with something less expensive.

For photo editing, you can easily begin with one of my favorites. It is called PhotoSuite. It came free with my scanner many years ago. The software was worth the cost of the scanner (and lasted a lot longer as well). I have version III. At the time this book went to print, the latest version was PhotoSuite 5 Platinum. The retail price is only about $50. This software enables the user to eliminate red eye, scratches, and otherwise enhance the photos. It is an excellent starter program for photo editing, in my opinion.

You will most likely want some type of image editing program like this. There are many out there. This one is my favorite mostly because it was free and extremely simple to learn. Within about five minutes, I was creating photo shirts and mousepads with it. I wouldn't hesitate to recommend it for the current retail price. I use it for almost every photo transfer that I create.

One word of caution... although many of these applications come with built-in free clip art and offer the ability to add text to a photo, make magazine covers, etc., please be sure to carefully read the license agreement with whatever application you do get. Some do not allow you to use their graphics for commercial (for profit) use. I strongly suggest you make sure of the approved usage prior to buying a package.

The only other substantial caution that I want to mention is that you should carefully watch the quality of the text that you add to a graphic or photo; if you're not careful, the text quality when you print the design might not be as good as you're expecting. As you will read in the following paragraphs, when you work in photo applications, you are working with a format called *raster*. When you work in programs such as Corel Draw, you are working in a *vector* program.

I highly recommend that, as you are able to afford it, you consider using both applications to create the best combination of artwork for your custom products.

You can edit your photos in a photo/raster program. Then you open your vector program and import the edited photo into it. Now when you type your text, you can resize it without fear that the quality will be degraded.

The ability to print clear text and graphics onto a sheet of transfer paper is vital as you begin build your reputation. It is what will set you aside from others who are trying to do the same thing... make money making personalized stuff!

First, let's quickly go over some of the terms you'll need to know and figure out what equipment you'll need.

A5 » The Equipment – A Closer Look

Raster vs. Vector

What in the world is a **raster** or a **vector** you might ask? This distinction can very likely be confusing at first but it will become much more clear as you work with both formats.

Images that come from an image editing or painting program will generally be raster images (also called bitmaps). JPG, TIF, GIF, and BMP are all examples of raster image formats.

A **raster image** is made up of a series of small dots or pixels which together form a complete picture. Raster images typically come from scanners, digital cameras, and/or photo editing or paint programs. Raster images are ideal for photographic and very complex images but the file sizes are often much larger than those of vector images. They also don't usually scale very well.

For example, if you were to type your name in a raster program and then enlarge it to several times it's original size, it's very likely that the words would become "pixilated" and difficult to read. The edges of the letters that appeared smooth at their original size will have turned into jagged boxes of colors and tints.

A **vector image** is made up points, lines, and curves, and the geometry and mathematics that determine how those vectors will be represented. EPS, WMF, CGM, and SWF are all examples of vector image formats.

If you used a vector-type program, like Corel Draw for example (I know I keep mentioning this program but I promise I don't work for them... grin), you could type the same name, enlarge it to several times its original size, and the quality would not change at all. Vector images appear exactly the same no matter how large or small they are displayed.

A vector application is something you can add later if your budget doesn't allow for it now, but I highly recommend that you consider purchasing one when you are able.

Cindy
RASTER – ORIGINAL SIZE

Cin

RASTER – ENLARGED 800%

Cindy
VECTOR – ORIGINAL SIZE

Cin

VECTOR – ENLARGED 800%

A5 » The Equipment – A Closer Look

Heat Press

Now we're getting to the good stuff. There are several types of presses and more than a few brands and manufacturers. While some of these press companies have an excellent reputation, most presses will do essentially the same thing.

Some have special manufacturing that is supposed to allow them to heat more evenly while others will come with other "bells and whistles" designed to make your job simpler.

I recommend that you purchase the press with the largest heating area that you can afford. I was on a very tight budget when I started in this business and decided to start with a small press called a JP14. It was a fine press but I realized within the first couple of weeks that, for what I wanted to be able to do, that I would need to have a larger press.

You heat press will likely be your most expensive single purchase for your new business so please make this purchase carefully.

You will need to determine for yourself if you are the type of person who needs the bells and whistles. Yes, they do make things simpler, but do you need them if money is tight?

I don't pretend to know what is best for you and your own situation so please take what you read here as a starting point and then make your own decisions.

I personally believe that you should buy the largest press that you can afford. Why? Because if you do what I did and later realize that the press you bought is just too small for your needs, you'll likely regret your original purchase.

You might have to sell your nearly new press (probably at a loss) like I did mine. You might decide to keep it as a backup press in case your new press fails you. This is a good idea if you can afford it, however new presses don't often break down, so now that first press could be money in your pocket rather than a useless accessory sitting in a garage or closet collecting dust.

If you do find yourself with an extra press and are able to hang on to it, you may find that in an emergency having that second press around can sure keep you in business and generating income rather than waiting for parts or a replacement.

The best situation when you first start up your business though would be that you simply avoid making a mistake on your heat press purchase. Most vendors don't mind having you ask questions and can give you a lot of valuable information. If they seem irritated with you for wanting to be cautious with a major purchase, you should probably consider buying from a different vendor. Your heat press purchase will be crucial to your new business. Don't let yourself be rushed into a decision if you're not comfortable with it.

Here are some questions to ask a potential vendor about presses that you're considering:

1. **How large is the heating area?** Most, if not all, heat presses have an area along the edges of the platen that shouldn't be considered part of the heating area because the outermost edges usually don't heat to the full temperature. On average, it's safe to estimate

A5 » The Equipment – A Closer Look

approximately 1/2"- 1" on each of the 4 sides that will not be reliable enough for a consistent temperature.

So, for a press that measures 9" x 12" on the heat platen, the realistic area could be as low as approximately 8" x 11". A smaller press will obviously have a lower price but remember that if you will be making shirts with commercial/stock transfers, that many of these can be up to 15" x 15" in size.

If you are pretty sure that you will not ever want to do a transfer larger than a sheet of regular letter sized paper (8 1/2" x 11"), a 9" x 12" might work fine for you.

I hear of many people starting with a 15" x 15" heat press. This is a pretty safe and still fairly economical size to start with if you're on a tight budget. It will easily do the letter and even legal sized transfers as well as many of the commercial/stock transfers.

My personal opinion on press size though is that if you can afford it, and are fairly confident that you'll stick with this new business of yours, that you get a 16" x 20" heat press.

The main reason I recommend this is because that size press will do the commercial/stock transfer sizes. Also, in a world where fewer people actually wear a size "small" anymore (I sure don't), you will probably find that the most common sized shirts you'll need to press will be XL or 2X. A smaller press than a 16" x 20" could make it difficult to easily align your blank shirt on the press so that you'll get an even transfer.

An additional reason is that typically, though not always, a 16" x 20" press will have more of the conveniences than some of the smaller presses do: the timer, the temperature dial that is usually a little simpler to set and simpler to read (and possibly a little more accurate).

If you plan to add dye sublimation (for mugs and other items) to your line of products, you'll need to make sure that your press can reach temperatures of at least 400 degrees. Some of the smaller presses are not made to heat to that degree so they will not compatible with the dye sublimation method. This might not be something that matters to you now, but if you change your mind and add dye sublimation later, you'll have to upgrade to a different press at that time.

2. **What is the warranty?** A standard warranty can range from one to three years. The main thing to be aware of is that it is at least a one year warranty and that the company has a reputation that you feel a level of comfort with if you should run into a problem with your press.

3. **Is the press I want in stock?** If not, what is the expected shipping/delivery schedule? Many vendors do not stock the presses they sell. This is not necessarily a bad thing. It might even work in your favor. If a vendor doesn't have to pay to have a press shipped first to their location and then to yours, that could possibly save you some money off the retail price.

4. **How much is the shipping cost?** Heat presses are very heavy. That means higher costs than you might expect for shipping charges. Make sure you account for shipping in your budget.

You might have additional questions and that's fine. Make sure you get all these questions answered to your satisfaction before you part with your money.

Types of Presses
- **Flat**
- **Cap**
- **Mug**
- **Other**

The most common type of press is the **flat press**. This simply means that the heating area is flat. The presses that I have described in the first part of the book have all been flat presses.

You use a flat press to press... well... flat things. Items such as t-shirts, mousepads, puzzles, tote bags, aprons, and the list goes on. This is the type of press I would recommend for your first press purchase because it will give you the most flexibility and all you to make the widest variety of products.

As you grow your business, or if you believe that you will be selling enough ball caps to justify a second press from the start, you can consider adding a cap press.

A **cap press** is smaller in size, the heat platen is rounded to fit the size and shape of a ball cap. You should know that there are different 'profile' sizes for cap presses. You will want to ask your vendor which profile attachment(s) are standard and which are available as add-ons with whichever cap press you decide to purchase.

Caps are super fun to make, and the profit on them can be as healthy as the profit on shirts, but be aware that, with a cap press, you will make only caps. I have a cap press and love being able to make caps for customers but I probably only sell one cap for every dozen shirts or other flat items.

A **mug press** is even more of a specialty press than a cap press. They're primarily for niche markets but there is no doubt that the cute mugs with sayings and photos on them are just precious and can be profitable as well.

Be aware though, that to make mugs, you have to use a dye sublimation process. This requires entirely different inks, a separate printer for those inks, a color profile to help the colors print correctly, a different type of paper, and a learning curve that can be very frustrating at first.

That said, once you've got your dye sublimation setup working properly in addition to your other system (as focused on in this book), it's an awesome process that will open your product line up to many other items as well.

Dye sublimation is a great second/add-on process in my opinion, but I have to admit, it was very frustrating for me at first, so I'd recommend waiting until you're comfortable with the pigmented ink process before branching out into sublimated products.

If and when you do add dye sublimation, and if the costs of mug presses are too high for you, there is another option that may save you some money. It is called a **mug wrap**. These are small wraps that go around the mugs and are baked in an oven instead of heating them in a mug press. The prices are about $30 for a mug wrap setup compared to several hundred dollars for a mug press.

Other types of presses do exist, label presses for example. They are much less common and are essentially very small flat presses with prices that may or may not be equally small. I don't have any of these presses and, unless you have a specific need for one, I'd recommend skipping them, at least for now.

New vs. Used

I'm often asked if I believe that a used press is a good idea. That's something that you'll have to determine for yourself. I will tell you that the second press I bought (when I sold my first press because it was too small) was a used press that I found on eBay. I was very new to the business at the time and didn't realize the potential risks of buying a used press.

It took me about a month or more to get my 16" x 20" used heat press. When I asked about the delay, the seller told me that they had personal issues and reasons for not shipping it on time. I remember thinking, with a horribly nauseous feeling in my stomach, that I had just lost $600+ dollars.

Eventually, I did receive the press after several emails to ask for tracking numbers, etc. and I'm happy to say that my press is still healthy and working quite well several years later.

If you are considering a used press or need to sell a press so that you can upgrade; be sure to visit our online forum at http://press2success.com/imadethat/. We have a free classified section there so you can see if there are any used presses available at the time you are ready to make your purchase.

Buying used can definitely be a money saver, but you'll usually have to put your trust in a person you've never met. With any large purchase like a press, and after hearing some of the horror stories I've been told about bad presses that were purchased used, I personally would prefer to go with a new press and have that warranty in my possession. Again, go with your gut instincts and your budget to make the best decision for yourself.

Brands

There are at least a handful of brands out there. I can't honestly say that one is the best or one is the worst. Within each brand, there are different models and sizes. My best suggestion is to ask around on Internet user groups to see what brand names and models you hear the most positive information about.

Costs

Depending on the size, brand, and type of press you buy, you can expect to pay anywhere from $250 to $2500. I know this is a very wide range of prices and features and is the biggest reason that I recommend that you really do your homework before making your decision.

Home Irons

Every time I have someone ask me if they can just use their home iron, my heart sinks. I want to tell them, "NO; don't use a home iron. You'll most likely lose more money in ruined attempts than you'd have paid for a small entry press."

I don't usually say that when I'm asked, though. Why not? Because I know that until a person finds out for themselves what they can't do, it probably doesn't matter what I say.

Can you do heat transfers with a home iron? Yes, truthfully, yes. Will the results be consistent? Professional?

A5 » The Equipment – A Closer Look

Provide even pressure? Not hurt your arm? No... Most likely they will not. A few people have had some degree of success with a home iron but the majority quickly realize that they really do need a professional press to produce a professional product.

I hope that this explanation will save you the trouble of even trying but if you feel it's something you have to see for yourself, you're definitely welcome to experiment with one. I am also a person who has to make my own mistakes before I can really believe whether something can't or shouldn't be done so I completely understand that line of thinking.

If you do try a home iron and produce what you think is a successful product, please put it through a battery of washes. You'll need to test the expected life span of the transfer. Most transfers look incredible when they're first made. If they're not made with a nice steady pressure however, they may begin to crack prematurely regardless of the paper quality. A few washes and drying cycles will probably tell you all you need to know about using a home iron to produce heat transfers.

I realize that we covered heat presses pretty extensively here but I recommend that you take your studies even further before you make your purchase decision. This will probably be your most expensive equipment purchase and you want to make it wisely.

Printers

Now we're back to smaller price tags and slightly simpler decisions. You only have a couple of options as you get started. The first option is not one that I recommend but it is a possibility if you're on a very tight budget.

Any Existing Printer and OEM Inks

There are some people who make transfers using their existing printer and the inks that came with that printer. This method is fine and dandy for a hobbyist or for making items that will not be washed.

You could make mousepads, puzzles, and possibly ball caps with your existing printer and inks. As long as you stay clear of washable items like shirts, aprons, and other articles that might be thrown in the washing machine, you can probably get away with it for awhile.

When you're ready to move on to washable items, however, I really recommend using a special ink that will work much better for producing a quality personalized transfer item.

Let's do a brief study of the different types of inkjet printers so you can understand why one brand is preferred over others in this industry.

Piezo vs. Bubble-Type Printers

There are a couple different types of inkjet printers, **piezo electric** and **thermal bubble**. At the time of this writing, Epson® is the primary manufacturer (if not only one) that uses the piezo method. The thermal bubble method is more commonly associated with printers from Hewlett-Packard® and Canon®.

Thermal Bubble Printers

This method of printing is performed by transistors inside the print head that create a small heating effect. The heat causes a bubble to develop. The bubble then pops, which is how the ink is disbursed. When the bubble pops, it creates a vacuum effect which will reload the print head with more ink. Bubble type printers use water-soluble, dye-based inks that typically won't be permanent when washed.

Piezo Electric Printers

This method of printing is performed, not by heat, but with crystals. An electrical current passes through the crystals which causes them to vibrate, pushing the ink out. The ink that was pushed out creates a vacuum which will reload the ink in the print head. Piezo type printers can use specialized inks as well as water-soluble dye-based inks.

When the Piezo type printer is paired with specialized inks, it can be used to produce permanent, washable transfers.

We can produce ideal transfers by using special inkjet transfer papers with a Piezo type printer that contains specialized inks which are specifically made for professional transfers.

As with many other technology products, printer models change so quickly that they are virtually impossible to specify accurately in a book. Within a short period, as little as a few months, many of today's models will have been replaced with new ones. Please investigate the models available at the time you are ready to purchase your printer.

Also be aware that at any given time, there are several manufacturers of transfer paper out there, trying to come up with a solution to the issue of only having one printer line that can be compatible with what we do.

I am constantly looking at and testing when I find potential additional solutions for our field. For the most recent product types, brands, and vendors to buy them from, please visit our forum.

As far as the Epson line though, which is where we stand right now, if you like, you may email me with the models you are considering. I would be glad to let you know if they will be compatible with the professional inks at that time. My email address is:

  cindy@press2success.com

And answer forum located at:

  http://press2success.com/imadethat/

Now that you understand why people in this industry prefer to use Epson® brand printers, we can discuss some of the ink types that we have to choose from. In order to avoid writing a book on all the brands of ink that are available, we will focus this section specifically on Epson® compatible inks.

Inks

OEM

OEM stands for Original Equipment Manufacturer and they are the standard brand name inks that are manufactured specifically for use with a particular printer by the company or by an agent for the company that sells the printers.

As I mentioned previously, some people choose to use their current printer and whatever OEM/brand name inks that are specified for use with that printer. If the OEM inks are dye-based, you could be setting yourself up for quite a bit of trouble.

Dye-based Inks

Dye-based inks frequently bleed and fade when they're washed. You may have seen some t-shirts or other items that were printed with dye-based inks and showed these unfavorable results.

When using dye-based ink on a shirt, you should assume that it will fade and/or bleed. These are not inks that I would ever recommend for use when making professional t-shirts or other washables. Can it be done? Yes. If your intention is to sell them for profit though, I wouldn't recommend it. Your reputation is the most important aspect of your business; guard it carefully.

The most deceptive thing about using OEM inks when making a custom personalized item is that they can look so awesome when they're first made. It isn't until after a few washes that you will notice the substantial deterioration of quality.

In a situation where you are on a very tight budget however, I do think that using your current inkjet printer, regardless of the ink type and/or brand with the OEM inks is acceptable on certain items. For example, puzzles, mouse pads, wall hangings, possibly even coasters or any other non-washables can be great starter products to help you generate some start-up cash.

You will probably find that one of the main products that people will ask you for as you begin your business is a basic t-shirt. If at all possible, you will want to set up your professional printing system as quickly as you can.

Pigmented Inks

Pigmented inks are a little different in their makeup. Basically, dye-based inks are like liquid with dyes added to color them, not too different from adding food coloring to icing for a cake.

Pigmented inks on the other hand are created by adding actual fragments of color to the ink base. The pigments, since they're not a liquid dye, will not fade by gradually washing out over the continued washes during the lifetime of the shirt/item. They will become permanently bonded to the product that you're producing.

It's because of these pigmented inks that we in the custom heat transfer industry have the success and professional results that set us apart from the others who use less professional supplies. If you're one of the people who have made things using OEM inks or even an inferior pigmented ink set, don't worry!

Almost every one of us started by using an OEM ink with an existing printer. We simply didn't yet know that there

A5 » The Equipment – A Closer Look

was a better, more professional option out there.

One extra word of caution... don't assume that if the ink claims to be pigmented, that it is completely pigmented. What I mean by this is that some inksets are indeed pigment-based, but might also include dyes as well.

If an ink includes any dyes at all, you are still running the risk that the shirts or other washables will bleed and/or fade. We use only pigmented inks in our products and have been extremely satisfied with the end product results. Even three years later, after washing approximately once a week, the items have held their colors with little to no noticeable fading.

Miscellaneous

One thing you might find within the Epson® line of printers is a line of inks that they call **DURA**Brite®. These are pigmented inks and are a much better option than dye-based inks. They are OEM and can be considered a potential option if you choose not to purchase a third party ink for whatever reason.

One thing that you will find if you opt to use this particular line of inks is that when the transfer is put into the heat press and is transferred onto a shirt or other blank, some of the colors may shift.

What I mean by this, for example, is if you printed a gray elephant on your transfer, you may notice that when it's transferred, the grays have turned to shades of greens. Green elephants could be pretty embarrassing in a product that you are planning to sell.

I don't mean to say that the **DURA**Brite® inks are not great inks. For their intended purpose, they're super.

When we try to use them for a purpose that they weren't intended, however, they can produce less than professional results.

I have heard that it may be possible to tweak the color output so that the color shifting will lessen and sometimes disappear. I personally do not use these inks though so can't speak with any first hand knowledge about how this is accomplished.

My suggestion is that if you find yourself having to use an ink other than a top quality (no dyes) pigmented ink... these DURABrite® inks will work better for you than a dye-based ink. Ideally, though, I recommend finding a pigmented ink set that has proven itself in the heat transfer industry over time.

Transfer Paper

Transfer paper is something that most people who are starting out might buy just because it says "transfer paper" on the label. Believe me, it is a mistake to do that.

Usually when people are getting started, they shop for their transfer paper at a local office supply store. I know I keep saying this, but for hobby use or personal and gift giving use, these papers might be considered acceptable.

However, when you are in business to generate an income, it's time to advance to a commercial/professional quality paper. Many times, you'll be surprised to find that buying these commercial quality papers are actually less expensive than the paper you can get at an office supply store.

Transfer paper needs to do a couple of different things for you. It contains a carrier that should be thin enough that it doesn't leave a heavy feel to it. It also needs to be thick enough that it forms a permanently bond between the product and the artwork.

If the paper you are using cracks, peels or feels too thick, you should immediately begin testing other papers. This is not something that you have to accept as the norm.

Of course, I didn't mention (but should have), that you first need to make sure you that you are carefully following the instructions that come with your transfer paper. Sometimes the most common problem with the paper may be that the user is not properly following instructions.

If at all possible, you want to purchase a sample pack of

transfer paper before investing in larger quantities. There are so many brands and manufacturers that you'll want to test which ones work best for you before investing too much money in any one paper.

Not all companies sell sample packs but I definitely recommend testing before purchasing as there are so many that might look "fair to acceptable." What you really want for your business is something that looks "very good to excellent!"

Types of Papers
Whites/Lights

The most commonly used paper is a standard 'whites' paper. It is what you will use for transfers onto white and light colored materials.

This process is very simple and the expected lifetime of a shirt made with quality inks, professional paper and correct techniques can last well over ten years (or as long as the shirt lasts).

At some point, you will probably find people who want to buy transfers on dark colored shirts as well, but the most common paper you will probably use is going to be for whites/lights.

Darks/Opaque

When you are ready to create transfers onto medium to dark colored blanks (shirts or other products that have no design on them yet), you will need to look for what is called an opaque paper. Opaque paper is essentially a material that you print onto and then peel away the

A5 » The Equipment – A Closer Look

backing material. You then take the remaining transfer and press it onto your shirt/blank.

When you take into consideration that the opaque paper is almost like a sticker that gets set into the material, it isn't much of a surprise that the expected lifetime of a shirt made with opaque paper isn't as long as the expected lifetime of a shirt printed with regular paper.

One other thing that you will obviously need for your business is artwork. I will cover that area later in the book but I do recommend that another necessary part of your main setup include a good, royalty-free set of clip clip art.

You will find it very handy, especially if you are not artistic. I recommend buying the largest collection you can afford. It is listed last as it is truly the least important item of the main set up. It is however, very helpful.

Well, there you have it! This information should get you well on your way to setting up your full, professional business. Remember, if you have any additional questions on the main setup, please visit our Internet forum:

http://press2success.com/imadethat/

You will find in this business that, while you may not be able to purchase quality supplies locally, it is not difficult to find what you need using the Internet. We will include many Internet suppliers' contact information and website URLs at the end of the book in the Supplies Directory.

Money Matters!

Assorted Product Ideas That You Might Want to Make & Their Approximate Retail Values!

Here are several product ideas that you can use as part of your brainstorming session to determine what other products you might like to add to expand your business beyond simply t-shirts. There are many other options as well, but these are some of the more commonly made items.

Pricing Thoughts

Remember when you set the pricing for your product line that you will be selling custom, personalized products. These are not something that your customers can easily purchase at a local discount store. Don't underestimate the value of your products.

Your goal is to charge the highest price you can for a top quality product while still generating the most possible sales.

Think about this for a minute or two. If you price a basic t-shirt at $18.99 and are selling about 5 per week, estimated profit might be around $14.00 per shirt. Your total profit from that one item in a week would then average $70.

What if you reduced your prices to $14.99? Assuming more people would be likely to purchase this item at the $15 mark than at almost $20, let's see what your profit would be if you now increased sales to 10 per week.

A6 » Money Matters!

$14.99 sales price x 10 shirts sold in a week= $149.90 minus the $50 cost to make 10 shirts leaves an approximate profit of $100 for that week for that one item.

You might be asking me, why would I want to do twice the work for less than twice the profit. You *might not* want to if you have a lot of time invested in each shirt or if you have a high demand item. That's up to you.

However, if your design is fairly simple and takes only a few minutes to create (average is about 10-15 minutes from creation of artwork to completion of sale), then I have found that selling more items, even if they bring in less profit per item, will increase overall sales and customer satisfaction.

You know about customer satisfaction, right?

Let's assume that every single customer you served is very happy with you and your product. Let's say that each of them recommends you to one of their friends who also becomes a customer of yours.

You can do the math on this. Do you want 5 happy customers or 10 happy customers who help generate even more business for you?

Especially if you run a home-based business and don't have a visible storefront to draw customers, word of mouth can be your biggest sales tool. Your first few happy customers can generate many more.

There are lots of things to take into consideration when determining your prices. First and probably foremost, you want to make money. You probably didn't buy several hundred to several thousand dollars worth of equipment just to break even, right?

It is vital to determine, often by trial and error, the best price for each of your products for your particular market.

Promotions

Promotions are another tool to generate additional business. I created a card for frequent customers. I charge them full price for the items they buy from me. They can order one or a dozen at a time. On payment for the 12th full price item, I "gift" them a free 13th item of their choice.

I do put a $15 maximum on it so that someone wouldn't be tempted to buy twelve $5 buttons and then ask for a $25 photo face doll as their free item.

Surprisingly, this has brought me more referrals than it has repeat customers. I thought this was odd, but apparently it made a favorable impression on the customers. So, even though they didn't have want to buy another product for themselves yet, having that Frequent Buyer Card in their purse or pocket with my business information on it, encouraged them to refer new customers to me. (I do not allow customers to transfer their Frequent Buyer points to new customers but no one has asked for that either).

Using a Frequent Buyer Card also has worked as I initially hoped it would; it brings repeat customers back to me. There are a few who make my business their first stop when shopping for gifts. They have made enough purchases to redeem their free items. In fact, one woman made sure that she got another card so I can bet I'll see her again and again.

A6 » Money Matters!

You can modify the program to suit your own needs, but I really do recommend some sort of 'thank you' program. Your happy customers can become your biggest asset!

Advertising

You might also consider advertising your business but advertising is a gamble sometimes. Before placing your ad, be sure that you have a business telephone number that is listed in the local phone book and be ready to answer it.

If people can find your number in the book or call information to get it, you know you won't miss any sales because someone lost your number. While you might not consider the telephone to be a form of advertising, it can make a big difference in your sales. Where is the first place someone will look when they want to find a promotional products business? The *phone book*!

And just having your number listed might not be enough. Who knows to look up "Cindy's Personalized Gifts" when they're looking in the white pages? It might be worthwhile to also place at least a small ad in the Yellow Pages section of your local phone book.

As far as newspaper ads and other forms of advertising, you may consider these possibilities, but be cautious. If you have a retail store location, it is much more realistic to expect these ads to work for you than if you have a home-based business.

For home-based operations, I would suggest you spend your advertising dollars on marketing through the mail or directly to groups such as schools, churches, etc.

Assorted Products with Approximate Retail Price Ranges

Understand this clearly; this is your business. There are no absolute prices that you have to or even should charge for your work. I will show an assortment of items that you might consider making and what I feel is an acceptable price range for retail sales.

What I refer to by retail sales include any sale where you sell directly to the end user. If this is a volume order for multiples of the same item, I personally would stay near the lower end of the range, based on the quantity. If you're selling only one item, I would charge closer to the high end.

Remember you are usually going to have to produce some custom artwork. When someone orders only one item, and it's not a stock item, you should be careful not to give your time away.

Wholesale orders may also come your way. These are items that are purchased by another business for the purpose of reselling. This could be for retail stores, schools or other fund raising groups. For them, you will want to arrange for reduced pricing whenever possible. After all, they will expect some kind of price break for a volume order. Be sure to take time to carefully analyze your costs and the profit you expect per job.

What I hear all too often (and I have done this a few times myself) is that we want to get that wholesale job because of the size of the order. However, in the pricing, we forget the cost of paper, shipping, or something else. Somehow we end up barely breaking even or even taking a loss when our time is added into the equation.

A6 » Money Matters!

Sometimes a screen printer truly is the best option for a particular job. I always recommend that a potential customer get a quote from a screen printer on orders of about 12 or more of the same artwork. That way my customer knows that I am not trying to get a job that could possibly be better done by someone else.

The trust that I built and the return of potential customers to my business who tell me that the screen printer was even higher than my bid (or they smoked, or they couldn't do photos, or they were going to be 2 weeks in production), can be invaluable to a business. There are so many situations that I hear about when they come back to me. It's not always a bad idea to refer a customer elsewhere.

You may also want to contact a screen printer or two in your area and work out some kind or arrangement where you would get a reduced cost for repeat business. Then, if you have a project that can be done better, cheaper, or faster by a screen printer, you can take the job, sub-contract it to the screen printer, and still make a profit while your customer pays the same price they would have paid if they'd gone directly to the screener.

Wholesale jobs are very nice to get as well. But don't give your products away just to move a larger quantity. Price them so that they will be worth your time. I typically try to price my wholesale orders at approximately 40-50 percent lower than retail. I usually require a minimum of 24 pieces ordered at a time, but allow a customer to mix and match products. That gives the reseller the ability to make a profit or even put items on sale if they don't sell well. As long as the reseller makes a profit, they will likely continue to reorder from you!

Estimated Retail Prices for Products

ITEM	RETAIL
Aprons	$12-$20
Baby Bibs	$8-$15
Ball Cap	$10-$15
Bandannas	$8-$15
Bumper Stickers	$4-$10
Buttons	$4-$10
Calendars	$8-$25
Can Coolies	$8-$15
Checkbook Covers	$8-$15
Clocks	$8-$15
Flying Discs	$6-$15
Greeting Cards	$4-$15
Journals (blank inside)	$8-$15
Kitchen Towels	$8-$15
Memo Cubes	$5-$15
Mouse Pads	$10-$15
Pet Apparel	$10-$20
Pet Accessories	$6-$20
Posters	$7-$25
Pot Holders (non-heat side)	$6-$15
Purses	$10-$50
Puzzles	$8-$20
Shorts	$10-$15
Sports Towels	$8-$15
Tote Bags	$8-$20
T-Shirts	$8-$20
Under Garments	$7-$15

The Other Systems

Ready to branch out?

There are several other systems that you can add to your personalized products business when you're ready. The great thing about this industry is that you can start with the custom heat transfers and as you gain knowledge and experience; you can add additional product lines simply by adding an extra piece or two of equipment and a few supplies.

Since this book is geared primarily toward heat transfers as a start up business, I will not go into details on these other systems. I would like to mention several of them however so that you can use some of the basic information in your business plan.

If you feel that you would want to produce several different products from the start of your business and believe that you would like to set up more than one system; this section should help you determine the basic equipment needs to assist you in purchasing what you need.

Remember that our Internet forum is available for updated information as well as interaction with others who are at various points in their own business.

Often times, it is interaction with others who are going through the same experience as well as others who have already completed their set up, that helps you avoid making costly mistakes.

You can find the forum at:
http://press2success.com/imadethat/
See you there!

Other Systems & Products

1) Dye Sublimation

2) Thermal Vinyl

3) Signs

4) Buttons

5) Photos

6) Glass Etching

These are just a few other systems that you can add to your abilities. Let's go into a little information about each of the systems and some possibilities. Because the first three listed above are systems that I personally find as staples to my business, I am going to include them in their own section immediately after the summary.

I'll cover buttons, photos, and glass now. These are great add on product lines that can be a great little sales builder. I wouldn't necessarily consider any one of them a business in itself though.

Buttons

I'm sure that everyone has seen the ads in the magazines when we were growing up about how you can make money making and selling buttons. Truth be told, I wanted one of those button makers all my young life!

I never got that button maker...until last year. You know what? I probably could have done without it another 35 years.

Don't get me wrong though, being able to make photo buttons has been a neat novelty product for me. Because

B1 » Other Systems & Products

of the lower price tag, it will attract people who might not have enough money set aside for a shirt or other product that has a higher price tag.

The nifty thing about button making is that one kit can make several different products. You can buy a very inexpensive button press for under $50. From the button parts that are available, you can make pin back buttons, magnets, keychains, and mirrors.

If you're looking for a low priced item to add and have realistic expectations about the volume of sales; a button press might be a good addition for you.

Photos

This is a very wide topic, one that I can't elaborate enough on here. You can print photos onto a wide variety of items. That's not really what I'm suggesting you add to your product line right now (hopefully you're already doing them on shirts).

Here, I am specifically recommending something that I added to my store just a few months ago. It hasn't generated a huge amount of sales, but it has been used for multiple projects.

I purchased a very specific printer (again Epson brand) that was created specifically for home use, but very professional quality photo printing onto a premium photo glossy paper.

For this printer, I do not use a third party ink, but use the OEM inks that are made for that printer. They make beautiful photos.

I have had several people coming into the store asking

me to scan their family photos and transfer them onto a white material so that they can make memory quilts out of them.

Quite often, these people will also ask me to print on photo paper additional copies of the cropped, retouched photos for family members (These are candid shots. Make sure that you don't copy professional photos without permission from the photographer to avoid copyright infringements).

In addition to photo prints above, I've found with the popularity of scrapbooking, that often people want a copy of a photo that they don't want to cut or alter. They have come to me to crop a section of the photo to enlarge it so they could have a better photo to include in their scrapbook.

Be sure to get a printer (I bought the R300 model) that has the ability to read and print directly from the media cards that digital cameras use. This is a handy option if you don't have a 6 in 1 type of media reader outside of the printer as well.

Again, similar to the buttons, this might not be a big money maker, but since it's a relatively low investment product line (the cost of the extra printer and photo paper...approx. $200), I think it has been an excellent addition to our offerings.

Glass Etching

This one is a neat little project that I believe had I invested in the professional level of equipment would have been a big success. I opted (for budgeting reasons) to go with a hobby store level of equipment.

B2 » Dye Sublimation

While I'm able to make glass ornaments with cute sayings like, "Baby's First Christmas" on it, the hobby level equipment is somewhat limiting as far as templates for text.

Since I do have a plotter, I also have purchased a mask material that allows me to cut out graphics and text onto the mask/material. I weed it just like I do for other vinyl like materials. Adhere it to the glass blank is the next step. This material is much better to work with as you can get a better adhesion to the glass blank.

The unit I have is a can of air with a spray gun attached to a jar of very finely ground sand. The sand is reusable, so the air can is the item that I have had to replace as a consumable.

The glass personalization is a very elegant product. It can be very simple or very ornate. There are clear glass plates, ornaments, even votive candle holders or shot glasses are your potential canvases for your glass art.

The hobby level of this equipment is in the ball park of $100. I haven't fully investigated the costs of a professional set up, but from what I have studied, it appears that the prices could range from several hundred to several thousand dollars.

If you feel you have a market for a more elegant product like etched/blasted glass products, this is a nice addition that can be learned very easily without much (if any) artistic ability necessary.

There are many other systems that you could add to your business as well. As you build your business, you will find more and more products and systems that you can add to your business to generate additional income.

Dye Sublimation
A Great Second System

Dye Sublimation is a process where the "dye sub" ink changes to a gas and impregnates the material, such as a mug, tile, shirt, etc. It actually becomes a semi-permanent to permanent part of the special coating rather than sitting on the top layer.

When done correctly, images printed with this system will be permanent. However, not all inks are the same quality and some may still wash out or fade over time.

In many ways, this process is very similar to standard heat transfer and sublimation products can be created with the use of an inkjet printer much like heat transfer. There are, however, some substantial differences too.

HT = Heat Transfer DS = Dye Sublimation	HT	DS
Works well with 100% cotton or cotton content materials	👍	👎
Can be used to make mugs, tiles, plates	👎	👍
Price averages $25 per 4 oz bulk bottle (or less)	👍	👎
Can be used with a special paper or carrier to work with dark materials	👍	👍
Depending on supplies used, can leave a slight "hand" or no feeling to it at all after washing	👍	👍

B2 » Dye Sublimation

You can see that there are benefits and drawbacks for each of these systems. I personally prefer heat transfers over dye sublimation for a couple of reasons.

Cost is the most obvious difference. Some dye sublimation inks can run in excess of $75 for a 4 oz bottle, while a quality pigmented ink can cost around $15-$25 for 4 ounces. The pigmented inks method can be very economical, yet still produce a high quality product.

I am in no way 'putting down' dye sublimation. In fact, I personally believe that the two should often be used side by side in a personalized products business. Since dye sublimation cannot be used with shirts that have a high cotton content, for example, I do all my shirts with pigmented inks and standard heat transfer.

On the other hand, if you want to make photo mugs or plates or tiles, you can't accomplish this without a good dye sublimation ink system. Yes, the costs are higher. If you want mugs though, a dye sub system is a necessity.

There are many other differences and pros and cons for each method, too many in fact to go into in much detail here. I would suggest however that if you want to print onto hard surfaces such as mugs that you do your homework and look into setting up an additional printer with these special dye sublimation inks.

Additional Equipment:

To add dye sublimation to your business, you will need to add an *additional printer*. The Epson brand will still work the best in most cases. Depending on the sublimation inks you choose, you might have a slightly more difficult time finding a printer that would be compatible with the dye sublimation ink cartridges. Remember that since these are typically all third party inks (for both systems), the vendors who sell the inks very likely have to purchase new empty cartridges and then fill them with their specialty inks.

This will usually limit the list of compatible printers to what they are willing or able to stock. It can be very expensive for vendors to try to stock every brand and type of ink cartridge. Be sure to choose your printer model based on its compatibility with the ink system you are planning to use (pigmented or dye sub).

In addition to another printer, you will of course need to buy *dye sublimation inks*. You can typically purchase the ink in pre-filled cartridges. If you like, you can also refill the cartridges yourself or purchase a bulk ink unit and bottles of bulk ink.

The bulk ink unit method will substantially reduce your cost per print over time. I have used the bulk method for years and absolutely love the cost savings and convenience. Without a good bulk ink system, you'll spend a lot of time refilling the cartridges which isn't particularly easy or fun.

One extra item that you may need to add for a dye sub setup would be a *color profile*. While some dye sublimation inks supposedly do not require a profile, I would ask for samples before purchasing the entire system.

Even if you do have the correct profile, there will likely still be some additional color management steps in order to perfect your color output.

If you've not heard of a color profile before, it's essentially a file that your computer will need to assist with color management. Your computer will use this file to

B2 » Dye Sublimation

help tell your printer how to deposit the right combination of inks onto the paper to reproduce accurate colors (many dye sublimation inks are initially set up with a different color formulation).

A special *dye sublimation transfer paper* is also highly recommended. It is possible to use a normal copy paper but the special paper will allow the dye sub inks to more effectively release from the paper and you'll get a much better final product.

The learning curve for this process is a little steeper but, once you have mastered it, dye sublimation can truly be an awesome companion system to pigmented transfers.

Thermal Vinyl

An Alternative for Colored Apparel

One nice option for customizing colored materials or very large items is something called *thermal vinyl*. This method essentially consists of a thin plastic material that is cut by a machine called a plotter (also called a sign cutter) and heat transferred to garments or other surfaces.

Thermal vinyl comes in a wide variety of colors and different parts of your designs can be layered on top of each other to create a dimensional effect. This method is commonly used for sports jerseys and other heavier, colored materials.

Unless sports uniforms will be a major part of your business, this is something you may want to consider adding to your product line later after your initial transfer business is running smoothly, as it can be rather expensive to set up.

Thermal vinyl can be an excellent addition to transfers but it doesn't necessarily give you the creative flexibility that digital transfers do.

Thermal vinyl artwork is limited to solid areas of color (the vinyl) and does not give you the option of printing photos or smooth gradations of color. To print photos onto dark material, all you need is your pigmented ink setup and an opaque paper.

When working with thermal vinyl, there are a couple of additional pieces of equipment that are necessary.

B3 » Thermal Vinyl

Additional Equipment required:

1) **Plotter:** You can start with an entry level plotter for as little as $500 while the larger (yet still considered small) units can be purchased for approximately $1400-$2000. There are many brands. Be sure to investigate your options fully. Small plotter costs are in the same range as that of a heat press and should be very carefully studied to avoid making a poor (and costly) choice.

2) **Heat Press:** I will assume that you already have a heat press for your transfer business but, if not, please refer to the heat press information in the equipment setup section.

3) **Thermal Vinyl:** This material is purchased in rolls, typically five yards or more in length. The width varies depending on what you need for your particular plotter. Common widths are 15" and 24". You can usually find other widths such as 10", 12" and 20" as well.

There are several different brands of thermal vinyl material available. It is a good idea to ask others in the industry which they prefer as well as performing your own testing to determine which is best for you.

4) **Teflon:** The only other item you really need is a teflon protective sheet that will act as a barrier between the thermal vinyl and the heat from your press.

There are also some much more expensive plotters ($8,000 to $30,000+) that function as printers as well as cutters. Most people in this business will probably not want or need them but they may be an option for later expansion of your business.

Thermal Vinyl is a great add-on. Give it some thought.

Signs

A Money Maker with Potential

Signs can be a super secondary income to those who are already making personalized gifts and apparel.

While the additional equipment can be a little more expensive than simply adding a single product or two to an existing transfer business, I believe you might find that the benefits are well worth the investment.

When I say signs, I'm not suggesting that you get a ladder truck or crane. I'm not saying you should set up a neon shop either. Leave the big stuff to the specialized sign companies.

What I am suggesting is that you may want to diversify your business to include small and temporary signage such as banners, 18" x 24" yard signs, automobile magnetics, and other small signs. This additional capability could be a great boost to your business due to cross-selling between the different product lines.

I found that customers would come into my store looking for a few shirts for their new business or to give as gifts. While visiting with them (or while they shopped in the store), they would notice one of my banners or signs. Often, that customer would call me later to ask if I could do a sign for their house that they just decided to sell on their own or for some other project.

If you choose to include signage in your business mix, I recommend also adding thermal vinyl since they both use the same equipment (other than the actual vinyl material used for each method).

B4 » Signs

One thing I found was that while many sign shops are already filling the market with their ads for "signs," "banners," and other products, there aren't many who market these items to the personalized product group.

If you drive by a sign shop or printer that has lettering or signs in their window, you'll see who they appear to be targeting. They usually market to small business owners who want signs or banners for a clearance sales or permanent signage.

What I did differently in my store was to make a sample 2' x 2' banner that simply said, "Happy 16th Birthday, Courtney." I used a very basic but fun layout, charged $22.99 and sold several just like it. All I had to do was to change the name and the birthday for each one.

Of course, the bigger sign companies could make birthday banners as well but they market to a different group of customers. I found a new niche and it paid off.

The message here is that you don't necessarily need to compete with more established sign companies. Find your own market and you can be successful too. Remember what you learned about niche marketing!

Additional Equipment needed:

Now that I've told you about how nice it can be to have signage as a companion product line to go with your heat transfers, let's talk dollars.

For signs, you will need to purchase a *plotter/cutter*. I mentioned this already in the Thermal Vinyl section. If you are leaning toward trying either thermal vinyl or signs, you should definitely consider adding both at the same time.

This could help you recoup the cost of the plotter more quickly and give you a few more things to experiment with in your product mix as well.

I began with a Stika 15" desktop plotter. It was very small but did the job and worked very well for me although I wasn't using it very much at the time.

When I began to get more and more demand for thermal vinyl shirts and uniforms, I realized I would need a much faster plotter. I decided to upgrade after only about six months to a 24" plotter. It is so much faster and quieter and has really been a joy to use.

As with your heat press purchase, the plotter you choose should be the best you can afford. If you have to start small and trade up, that is completely understandable. Just realize that you might end up taking a loss on the starter unit if you upgrade in a short time to purchase a larger, faster plotter.

There are several small accessories you will probably want to purchase to help produce signs: squeegees, a spray that aids in aligning the vinyl onto the surface material, cutting blades and so on. These extras can be very inexpensive but your main investment is going to be your plotter.

I really enjoy the variety of products I am able to make with my plotter. You don't necessarily need to start with a plotter/cutter in your initial setup but, as soon as you feel confident that you're going to do what it takes to make your business succeed, you may want to give it some serious consideration.

Quick Shopping List

You can use this page to help keep track of your shopping preferences. As you find your favorite brands and vendors for each of the items, jot them down here along with the URLs of the Web sites where you bought them.

Heat Press
Printer
Transfer Paper for Whites
Transfer Paper for Darks
Pigmented Inks
Blank Imprintables
Blank T-Shirts
Blank Totes, Caps
Thermal Vinyl, Sign Supplies

Tutorials

Getting started

Well, by this point, you've probably created your business plan, purchased or chosen your equipment and supplies, and now it's time to get started actually producing your personalized items!

I can remember how excited I was when I made my first few items. Of course, with the excitement sometimes comes confusion and the need to troubleshoot problems and figure out what you could have done better.

Remember that you will, without question, run into times when something goes wrong. Don't panic. Don't let it get you depressed. If you find that you need help right away, go to the Internet forum and usually within 24 hours (often much sooner), someone will have an answer for you.

This section will include "how-to" guides for:

Printers & Scanners	82
Aligning the Transfer	100
Transfers onto Whites	111
Transfers onto Light Colors	118
Transfers onto Dark Colors	123
Transfers with Thermal Vinyl	127
Transfers to Accessories	132
Transfers onto Other Blanks	136
Signs	139
Refillers Guide	145

You will find color photos from these tutorials on the Free companion CD inside the back cover of this book.

B6 » Printers & Scanners

Printers & Scanners

General Printer Information

I feel the need to preface this section with a couple of statements. First of all, I am not an Epson employee and in no way am I affiliated with Epson other than being a customer and owner of many of their printers over the years.

Secondly, the information provided in this book is gained from personal findings and is believed to be accurate. But please keep in mind that, since I do not own each and every printer model and regardless of what I believe to be true at the time of this writing, there are likely to be differences due to the speedy changes in technology.

That said, the best way to get accurate, up-to-date information on Epson printers is to visit the Epson website at

http://www.epson.com/

This section is included, however, to give you a general overview of the printers and scanners used in this business and show you specifically how to get the most from your equipment for your personalized apparel business.

What You Should Know
DPI and PPI

The first thing to learn about inkjet printers has to do with the printer's resolution which is measured in **DPI** or **Dots Per Inch**. The other variable that will affect your images is **PPI** or **Pixels Per Inch**. This is how your original images on the computer will be measured.

You don't necessarily need to know all of this but it might help you to understand how you can improve the quality of your printed pictures. The most important points will be in *italics*.

While the resolution of your printer is important to how your documents or transfers will look when they're printed, it is only one part of the equation. DPI can sometimes be misleading and also a little confusing, especially because sometimes when people talk about DPI, what they really mean is PPI. First, let's talk about PPI.

An image from your computer, whether it came from a scanner, digital camera, or straight from a "paint" or image editing program, is measured in **PPI or Pixels Per Inch**. The number of pixels per inch in your image is directly related to how your picture will look when it's printed and will affect how large you can successfully print that picture without losing image quality.

The most important thing to know is that, in general, the more pixels per inch, the higher the resolution, and the smoother (sharper) your transfer will look. However, there is a point at which any increase in resolution will make virtually no difference to the human eye.

For images on your computer, the ideal resolution for printing to paper is usually about 300-320 PPI at the final size you plan to print. Anything more than that and your file size will get larger but you probably won't be able to see any difference in the printed image.

To figure the ideal resolution for the original image, you multiply the width and height (in inches) by the number of pixels per inch. For example, if you have an image

B6 » Printers & Scanners

that you want to be 10" wide by 8" high, in order for that picture to be printed at the optimum 300 PPI, it would have to be 10 (inches) x 300 (pixels per inch) wide which is 3000 pixels in width. The height would be 8 (inches) x 300 (pixels per inch) or 2400 pixels high.

So, an 8" x 10" picture should be around 3000 x 2400 pixels for the best quality. What if your photo is only 1500 x 1200 but you still want to print it at 8" x 10"? Well, you may still be in luck because 300-320 PPI is the ideal resolution for prints on high quality paper such as a photographic paper. You probably won't need nearly that much resolution for printing a transfer that will go on a t-shirt because a t-shirt isn't able to display that kind of resolution anyway. *A resolution of 150-200 PPI is probably just fine for t-shirts.*

If your image isn't even large enough to give you 150 pixels per inch, you may still be able to enlarge it in your image editing program before printing. If the program doesn't enlarge images very well, there are other programs – some of them fairly inexpensive – that will do a better job of scaling images without sacrificing too much quality. Try looking online for image scaling (resizing) programs or ask someone in one of the online forums which program they use for this purpose.

The reason I said earlier that DPI can be misleading is because DPI does not correspond directly with PPI. A printer may put down several dots to reproduce one pixel of the original image. Inkjet printers in particular often use several dots for each pixel. This is because they're printing pictures with thousands (or even millions of colors) using only a few colors of ink. Most inkjet printers still use only four inks (cyan, magenta, yellow, and black). Some older printers may use only three colors of ink and some of the newer models are adding extra inks to try to produce a wider range of colors.

Anyway, *for most of our inkjet printers, the maximum or ideal resolution threshold is generally about 720 DPI* to produce a good print. 360 DPI is sometimes, but not always, good enough and 1440 DPI is usually overkill (unless you are using one of the newer chipped printers, which for some reason, seem to need the higher DPI setting to prevent banding on the printout). You should probably make a few test prints to judge for yourself. These are just recommended settings to give you a starting point.

If you were to print photos onto photographic paper, calendars, paper inserts for checkbook covers or basically any print that will end up on paper, a higher DPI setting will probably result in a much nicer quality print. Printer resolutions from 720-5760 DPI are not uncommon, depending on the printer you use.

Just keep in mind that each product and/or system will likely have it's own DPI range for best production results. You will learn these ideal resolutions as you experiment and gain more experience.

It isn't crucial to completely understand everything about image and printer resolution. You really only need to know which resolutions are important to your particular images and printer and these can be determined by trial and error or just by using our recommended settings of *150-320 PPI for images* and *720 DPI for your printer*.

Creating Transfer Settings

For the majority of this section, we'll be talking about how to set up your computer to print transfers using an Epson inkjet printer.

If you are using a different brand, some of this information will still be helpful. The majority of the set up tutorials however will not.

You should know that I am not excluding the other brands as a form of favoritism nor do I have anything against the other brands. For more specifics about why we use only Epson brand printers, please refer back to the printer portion of the section 'The Equipment - A Closer Look.'

Let's get started with how to set up your printer so that when you are ready to print transfers, you will not keep forgetting to flip the artwork to *mirror image*.

I am going to assume that you have installed the graphics software of your choice and have created your artwork. Now it's time to print it onto the transfer paper. Always read the instructions on your transfer paper before starting any project.

The images that I am using are for my CX5200 model. It is an all-in-one scanner/printer. It uses the C82 cartridges, which makes it handy because when one color runs out, you don't have to waste the other ink colors.

Remember though, if these images are not identical to yours, it might be simply that you have a different model. The process will be very similar however, so simply make the same changes to your own print settings.

1. **Start**: Begin by clicking on the Start button in Windows (we use XP) OS. The screen below should appear.

2. **Printers and Faxes**: Click on Printers and Faxes. This will bring the following screen.

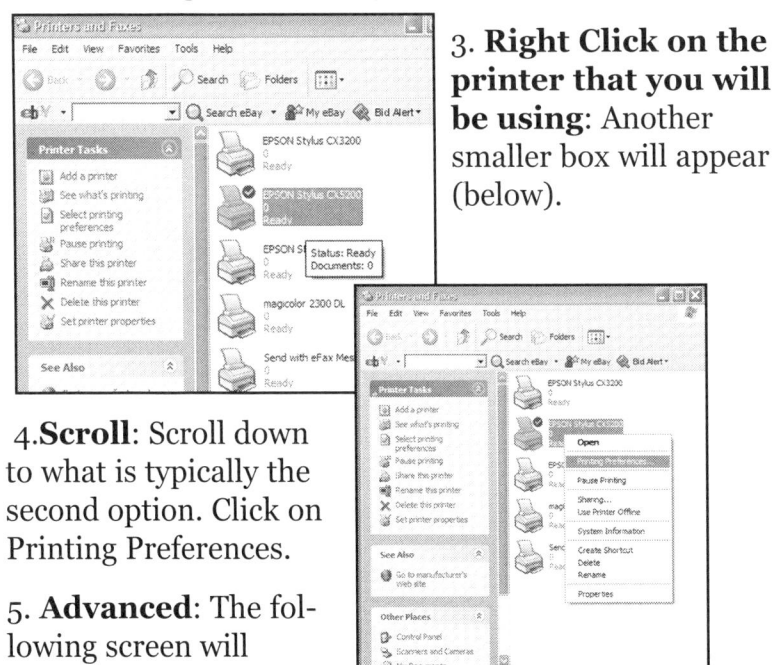

3. **Right Click on the printer that you will be using**: Another smaller box will appear (below).

4. **Scroll**: Scroll down to what is typically the second option. Click on Printing Preferences.

5. **Advanced**: The following screen will

B6 » Printers & Scanners

appear. This shows your current settings. These are likely your default settings. These will automatically be used if you click on the printer icon in most applications.

If you want your default settings to be the same as your transfer settings, simply set them as you would like them to be and click on OK at the bottom of the screen.

Since our settings for transfers are printed in mirror image, you probably will not want these to become your default settings. Most of us use a quality pigmented ink that is very good for transfers, but also is good for overall printing.

By doing this, we save ourselves from having to have two different printers (unless we have additional systems that require a dedicated printer).

I will assume that you want to add a printing profile for your transfers so that you can still do every day printing with the default settings.

Click on the *Advanced button.*

6. **Advanced Settings**: The screen that pops up now is for advanced settings changes. This is where we will need to make a few changes. Do not let the screen intimidate you. You likely will never have to adjust most of the settings on this section.

« 88 »

7. **Settings**: I will now assume that you will be using 8 1/2" x 11" transfer paper as we adjust the settings.

In the *Paper & Quality* section, I recommend leaving it at the plain paper setting. If the transfer paper you choose is a very thick paper, you might consider heavyweight matte, but most of us stick with the plain paper setting.

The next box gives you options for your print quality. It ranges from Economy, Normal, Fine, Photo to Best Photo on my printer.

Note: Some printers use DPI numbers such as 360, 720, etc. Still others simply use speed options. The 1280 printer uses the speed options on the basic settings page, but on the advanced tab, it shows the following: Economy, Normal 360, Fine 360, Photo 720 and Photo 1440.

For transfers, you might be able to use the Normal setting, but I personally stay with Fine, which usually helps keep banding problems to a minimum.

There is nothing wrong with using the higher DPI settings as long as you're using a quality ink that will not bleed. You should realize though, that using a higher DPI setting will usually result in a heavier 'hand' or feel of the transfer on the shirt. It's always a good idea to use the lowest DPI you can without reducing the quality of

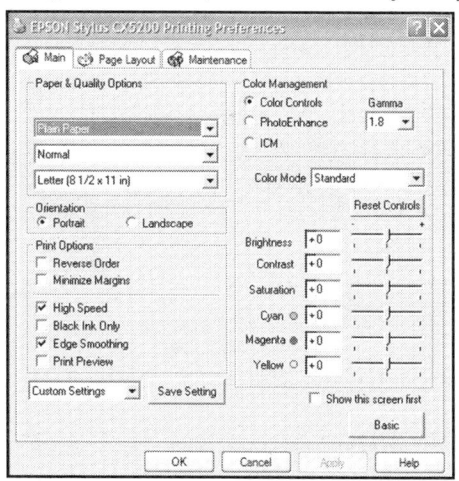

« 89 »

B6 » Printers & Scanners

the finished product. It may save you some ink too.

The third box in the Paper & Quality section is your paper size. If you would rather use the legal sized transfer paper instead of letter sized, simply change this to 8 1/2" x 14".

The *Orientation* section is pretty clear. If you want to print as you would in a letter, keep it on portrait. If you want a print that's wider than it is tall, that is called landscape.

I personally use more landscape than portrait prints. You can create a profile for each of them but, for now, choose the one that you think you would use most often.

At this point, you are finished on this screen. If you are comfortable tinkering with the settings for specific projects, please feel free to do so later. For now, you will not need to make any other adjustments in this area.

8. **Page Layout**: Do not save your changes yet, but click the Page Layout tab at the top of the screen. This takes you to the following screen.

The only thing you'll need to adjust on this screen is to place a check mark in the box at the top right that says Mirror Image. Once you have checked this box, click back to the original

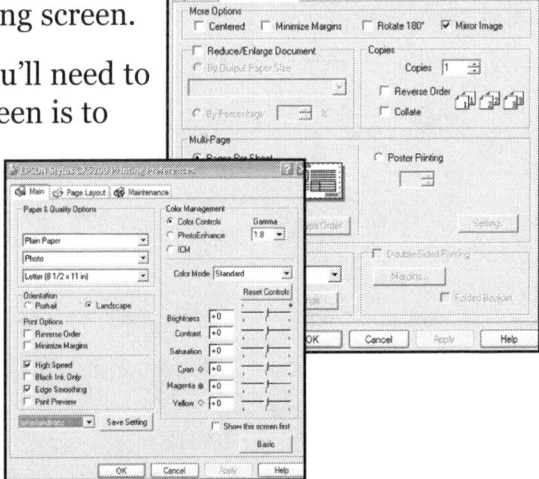

« 90 »

Main tab (where we just were).

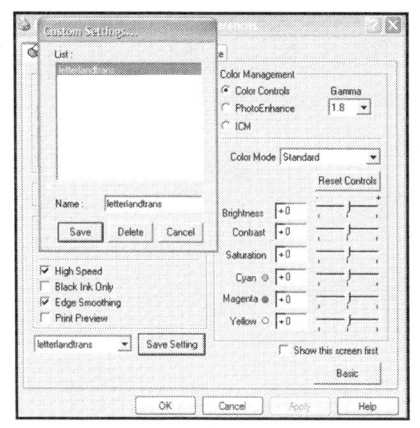

9. Save: Click on the Save Setting button at the bottom.

10. Type: When you see the box below, type a name or keyword that you will know is for your transfers. I used letterlandtrans on mine. It's short for Letter, Landscape, Transfers. This will let me know when I am ready to print a transfer that this setting is created for letter (8 1/2" x 11") sized paper, it's pointing sideways, and it will print at a slightly higher DPI and will print in mirror image.

11. Save: Now click Save and you've just created your transfers settings. Exit.

When you are ready to print your transfers, simply click on the File tab at the top of your window and scroll

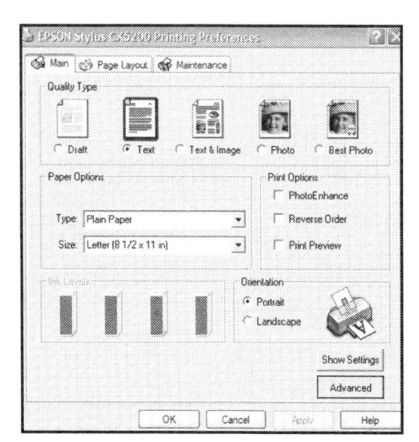

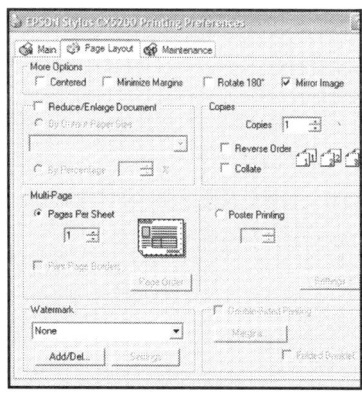

B6 » Printers & Scanners

down to Print.

When the general box appears, click Advanced, then click on your newly created *letterlandtrans*, then click on OK. Now what you print will be using those settings.

Print Nozzle Check

You might have picked up on a term called banding. If you don't yet know what it is, you will probably learn it soon from experience. Essentially, banding is inconsistencies in the printing process.

When printing with pigmented inks or sometimes if you don't use your printer on a daily basis, you might find that at occasionally there will be a deterioration of quality in your print. This is likely banding.

There is a very short and easy way to find out if this is indeed what is going on. Don't forget that it might also just be that you are running out of a certain color of ink. Check your ink monitor levels to see if that is the case.

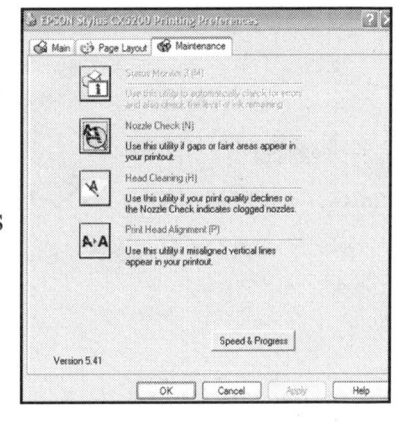

Assuming you are not out of ink, let's find out if you are having banding problems and will need to do a quick process called a print head cleaning.

In the same method that you got to your printer preferences screen (Start, Printers and Faxes, right click your printer, click on Printing Preferences), navigate your way to the screen shown above.

Cindy Brown » I Made That!

This will be the third tab rather than the first two that we just worked in. It is usually called the Maintenance tab. It is also called the Utility tab in some other models such as the 1280 and located in the fourth position, so you might need to search a little for it depending on your particular printer.

Usually, if you have a problem, you will need to check this screen to see if you can troubleshoot the problem.

1. **Nozzle Check:** Click on the Nozzle Check button. This will help us find out if some of the print head nozzles are plugged.

2. **Print:** When you click the Nozzle Check button, it pops up another smaller box. Here you have an option to either Print or Finish. For now, we want to click on Print.

If we clicked Finish, it would have closed the box and let us return to work.

3. **Check and Finish or Retry**: After you have given the printer time to perform the nozzle check print, it will

« 93 »

B6 » Printers & Scanners

send you a paper with bars on it as shown on the left.

Use this sheet to determine if you need to do a print head cleaning or not.

Even before trying the Print Head Cleaning, if the Nozzle Check shows that all bars are not printing, I like to try increasing my DPI setting one or two steps.

We will assume that raising the DPI slightly doesn't help, and we need to do a Print Head Cleaning.

Print Head Cleaning

Thankfully, doing a Print Head Cleaning isn't nearly as difficult or time consuming as cleaning your car. It is something that you might find yourself needing to do on a monthly, weekly, or even daily basis depending on the amount of printing you do.

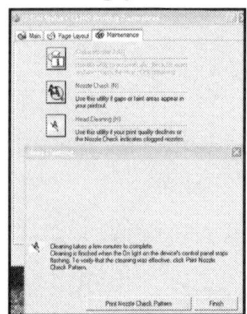

Again, from that same entry screen in your printing preferences, go to your Maintenance tab. Click on Head Cleaning. At this point the smaller box to the right will show up.

Click on Start. The cleaning takes a few seconds.

When the head cleaning has finished, you will see another box asking if you would like to print another

Nozzle Check. Do it.

If you still don't appear to be getting complete color bars, you can repeat it as necessary. Make sure to check the manual and Epson's website about this too. You could damage your printer by doing too many print head cleanings in a row. You might want to do just one, followed by a Nozzle Check; then if it still isn't printing properly, wait about fifteen minutes, and try again.

Purge & Prime
Purge

Usually, when you change cartridges, it will be useful to verify that you have gotten rid of the previous inks. We recommend using purging cartridges if you want to change from one ink type to another one.

What are purging cartridges and how do I use them?

Purging cartridges serve a couple of different purposes. One, of course, is to clean your printer of a previous ink type in preparation for you to put in a new ink. The other purpose is that if you find yourself with a clogged system, a purging cartridge could very possibly help you clear it up and get you back into production again.

These little cartridges (carts for short) are very handy to have around. You don't absolutely HAVE to have a set, and if you're low on funds, this is one item that you could possibly wait to get (keyword... POSSIBLY).

If you are changing your printer from one type of ink to another, such as from dye sub to pigmented, or vice versa, you really don't want to risk mixing the inks together inside your printer which could ruin your

B6 » Printers & Scanners

printer or send you on a trip to the repair center.

If you have a brand new printer, you will obviously not need to use these cartridges to cleaning one ink out and put in the new inks, but you might still want to have a set around as an "insurance policy" in case you get a clogged unit while working on a deadline.

How do I purge inks?

Purging cartridges are very simple to use. Make sure that any time you remove cartridges from your printer that you replace them as quickly as possible. You don't want to give the print heads time to dry out. If you're going to have open cartridges outside of the printer for more than a couple of minutes, you also might want to tape them shut or put them into a zipper bag to avoid letting them dry out.

1. **Remove** previous cartridges and put aside (or in a sealed bag).

2. **Verify** that you can see a small amount of clear liquid through the holes on the bottom side of the cartridges. Place purging cartridges into printer.

3. **Increase** the DPI to the highest setting available. Print one or two of the purge pattern pages (found on the companion CD).

4. **Run** two or three print head cleanings and then attempt to run several pages of printing. At first you will likely see some color and then nothing. This is what's supposed to happen. The color you see is the ink that was left in your printer. When you don't see it any longer, that means it has run out.

(Note: You should verify that you see a 'wetness' on the

paper, so you'll know that you've successfully purged your printer. If you don't see the moisture, try printing a few more pages mixed with a print head cleaning or two to make sure you are getting a proper purge.)

You're done! Take the purge carts out, put the ink system or cartridges back in and you're off to the races!

Prime

If you use third party inks, getting new cartridges to print successfully can sometimes take a little extra work as well. The process for doing this is located in the Q & A section at the back of the book.

It is important that you let the printer process your cartridge changes since it performs a 'charge.' This will greatly reduce the time needed to prime the printer compared to attempting to prime it manually.

I hope this printer section has been helpful to you. There are several differences from one printer model to another so feel free to post to the Internet forum with any specific questions you might have.

Make sure that you bookmark this location as it can be a wonderful resource for you as you get up and running.

http://www.press2success.com/imadethat/

Don't Forget About Scanners

A scanner can be an important piece of equipment in the personalized products business. It isn't necessarily required but, considering the reasonable cost and the benefits a scanner can provide, I highly recommend that you get one. Or an all-in-one printer/scanner combination might be an excellent addition to your business.

B6 » Printers & Scanners

Keep in mind that the all-in-one products will probably not be compatible with a bulk ink unit. If you plan to use a bulk ink system (highly recommended for medium- to high-volume users), you might want to purchase a scanner separately or, better yet, purchase an all-in-one unit to use as a backup printer.

DPI Again

There's that term again. I have to admit that I'm not a high-tech graphic artist. That's nothing to be ashamed of, and I'm not.

The good news is that you don't have to be one either in order to be successful in this business. You can easily learn as you go along in this business. That's one of the best things about of this type of work, in my opinion.

That said, this part may confuse you. When dealing with inkjet printers, we commonly use DPI settings of 360, 720, 1440, and so on. However, when dealing with scanners, you may see settings like 72, 300, 600, etc.

As I was learning the business, sometimes I just had to tell my analytical side to shut up and accept that whether I understand it or not, that's just the way it is. I don't always *need* to understand every detail; I just need to understand how to create a darn good product!

As far as what we *need* to know, here's what I recommend: *Scan your photos and graphics at 150-200 DPI* if you are going to be keeping them approximately the same size on your printout.

If you plan to increase the size of the printout as much as twice the size of the original, scan it at a higher DPI and see how that works.

If you want to print a photograph or other continuous tone image on photographic paper or other non-transfer item, where you want to have the highest clarity possible, consider scanning at 320-400 DPI. For line art, where the image is strictly black and white (no shades of gray), you'll want to scan the item as high as 1200 DPI.

Aligning the Transfer

You've Got it, Now Where to PUT It!

Aligning your transfer can be a very simple thing. Some people never measure the placement and have a knack for 'eyeballing' it. Some find it absolutely necessary to not only measure but will even have a template to keep their transfers straight. Regardless of where you fit in between these two extremes, rest assured that with some practice and basic understanding, you'll soon be able to have a high success rate aligning your transfers. Don't get frustrated if your first few don't look straight — it happens to everyone in the beginning. You'll get the hang of it soon.

If you are doing a single item, eyeballing can be a very simple method (as long as you have a straight eye). When you begin to take orders for multiple items with the same artwork, it might be time to consider taking some measurements. The reason for this is that you need to provide a consistent product for your customer.

This isn't rocket science but there is a little bit of logic involved. Remember that since most t-shirts are non-gender specific, both men and women, boys and girls (and maybe even a pooch or two) will be wearing these shirts. A woman's body is different than a man's and so forth.

If you know in advance that the shirts are going to be just for women or men, you might be able to customize the placement to better suit the particular body type. Overall though, the size of the shirt will best determine where you should place the transfers.

We will cover the placement of transfers for several different locations on a garment. You will have customers want to put designs in some of the strangest places. That's okay. That's why they came to you in the first place, to get a custom personalized product.

If you don't find the location or guide you are looking for below, simply use logic and determine where you think it would look the best. If it's an uncommon location, I recommend that you consult with the customer prior to producing the item so that they will be in full agreement with you about the placement. Maybe you could make one sample for their approval.

Ready? Let's get started!

Short Sleeve T-Shirt Pocket Front

A very common location for the front of a shirt is called a pocket print. Assuming there is no pocket on the shirt, the placement would be approximately 8" down from the top of the shirt.

I start at the collar (using my hand as a guide) and measure down approximately 8".

Typically, this will land just to the left of the armpit area.

On larger shirts (from 2X on up), you will find that the print will need to be placed just off center between the sleeve and the collar (slightly more toward the sleeve than the inside of the shirt). You may also

B7 » Aligning the Transfer

want to increase the size of the pocket print transfer for larger sizes and reduce the size of the transfer for smaller ones.

This will make your shirts look much more professional than using 'one size fits all' transfers. It might take a few seconds longer to resize them, but should increase customer loyalty as well as getting you some great referrals.

In cases where the shirts do have pockets, you will figure proper placement based on a couple of criteria. If the artwork is just a name or small logo, it should probably go right above the pocket.

If you'll be transferring a graphic or combination of picture and text, I typically will place the art directly on the pocket. One thing I have noticed in my area however is that I don't get many requests for pocket Tees, maybe only about one in every fifty shirts.

Short Sleeve T-Shirt Full Front

Probably your most popular transfer will be the full front design. It is usually centered below the collar of the shirt. I typically measure about four fingers/inches down from the bottom of the collar. If the design is not equally distributed I would recommend aligning the center point of the transfer at about four inches from the collar. The most important thing to do as you are getting started is just to look at it before you press it. Use common sense and decide if you would want it there if it were for you.

The measurements are a guide, but definitely should not be taken as "gospel." See what works best for your business and for your customers.

I like to have a roll of *heat tape* handy so that I can tape a transfer down in the approximate location that I think it should be pressed. This allows me to hold the shirt up to verify that I am seeing it correctly while it's flat.

I use heat tape because it can tolerate the heat of the press so I don't have to remove the tape until after pressing (so the transfer doesn't shift on me). I usually don't need to use heat tape at all but when I come to an unequally distributed graphic, the tape is handy to have around.

Short Sleeve T-Shirt Front Bottom

These aren't nearly as common, but for some people who like to have their personalized shirts be a little different from everyone else's, this can be a nice option.

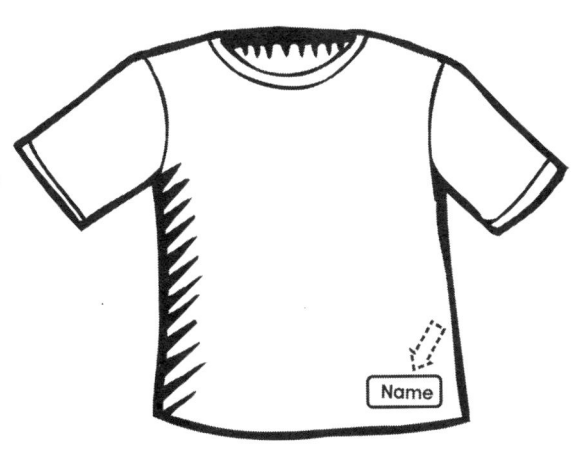

This location is often used for a person's name or for team names. It can be subtle or bold. I don't normally recommend combining this style with another print on the front although it's entirely possible to make combined transfers blend well together with a little thought

B7 » Aligning the Transfer

and effort. Of course, you'll be able to charge a little extra for this special service.

Short Sleeve T-Shirt Sleeve

You might find, especially in business or teamwear shirts, that your customer wants to use a sleeve print location on a short sleeved shirt. This is a very nice touch, especially for a logo or mascot.

For this type of placement, you have a lot of room to play. If the transfer is just text or something small, I typically align it about 1" from the seam at the bottom of the sleeve. It creates a nice, subtle look.

However, if you are doing a logo, mascot or other larger graphic, I personally like it to be a little larger and then I align the bottom of the transfer over the center of the sleeve and about one inch from the seam.

Typically, I would not recommend using the entire sleeve area as that might look a little too crowded. Again though, with some creativity, you can make most anything look attractive.

Long Sleeve T-Shirt Sleeve

A very popular print location lately has been the sleeve print on a long sleeve shirt (even more so than on short sleeves). I would estimate that out of 10 long sleeved shirts that I print, about seven of them want a sleeve print. Some don't initially ask for it, but when I let them know that it's an option (for a couple of dollars more), they almost always opt to add sleeve prints.

One more thing to consider with sleeve prints on long sleeve shirts will be which direction to orient the text.

As you can see in the illustration, there are actually a couple of options. I have found that both are almost equally popular.

The text can be placed to read vertically or horizontally. Both are appropriate and it is purely a matter of preference on the customer's part. If you run horizontal oriented text along a sleeve, be sure to set it up so the printing will read correctly (not upside down) when the arms are straight out to the sides.

A long sleeve print can often work very nicely with both front and back prints without becoming too cluttered. I would advise sizing graphics appropriately though so that the shirt doesn't end up looking like a patchwork of designs.

B7 » Aligning the Transfer

T-Shirt Full Back

This is another very popular placement for artwork on a shirt. It is especially common for those who want a pocket-sized print on the front to add a larger design on the back of a shirt. I find that men more than women use this combination of print areas. Another common preference (though I am not trying to stereotype) is that women will typically ask for a large transfer on the front of their shirts while men often want the large print on the back. In my market, I've found that both men and women like the sleeve prints.

A back print is very simple to do. You should measure down from the center of the collar about 5" to the top of your transfer.

You'll also want to note, if possible, whether your customer has longer hair in back. If so, adjusting the transfer placement down a couple of extra inches will make it more visible as long as the transfer's not so tall that it disappears into the top of the wearer's pants.

If you're doing a hoodie (hooded sweatshirt), remember to adjust the placement down as well so it's not covered by the hood. Usually, depending on the size of the transfer, I will measure down at least 10" from the top seam to the top of the transfer.

What I really like to do with hoodies is to use the heat tape. I align the transfer as low as I can so it is entirely visible and still appears properly placed. This varies greatly on the size and shape of your artwork, so use your own judgement in this situation. When you hold the sweatshirt up, try to place the hood as it would naturally fall on a the person wearing it. Make sure that it is correctly aligned, then put it back in the press and do your transfer.

With these basics in mind, you can make adjustments to meet your customers while still creating professional quality apparel.

Aligning the blank on the press

It is very important to make sure that you align your blank garment evenly on the press as your starting point.

You should know that the size of your press has a lot to do with ease of alignment. When I first started, I purchased a 12" x 14" press. When I would transfer onto XL and 2X shirts, I found that while my garments were 'mostly' straight on the press, there were often minor problems in keeping them aligned.

When I moved up to a 16" x 20" press, I realized that the press really does have a lot to do with helping me align the shirt more evenly. Now I can use the press itself to help me align the shirt.

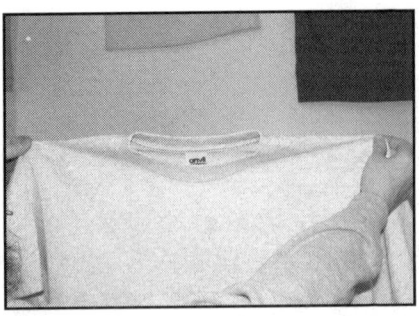

B7 » Aligning the Transfer

1. **Pinch**: Pinch the shoulder edges where the sleeves meet the body of the shirt. These are your squaring off points. Shake off any lint or excess fibers now as well.

2. **Align Top**: The next step is to align the top of the shirt with the press. To do this, you will take your pinched corners and place them equally on either side of the press. I took a marker and made a line down the center of my press (permanent so that it will not come off onto any apparel). You may want to do this too; be careful to get the mark exactly in the center.

Always double (and triple) check your alignment. Sometimes shirts are not made perfectly. At times, you will find that the center of the collar isn't the actual center of the shirt. If you do a double centering process, you should have the most success centering your shirt.

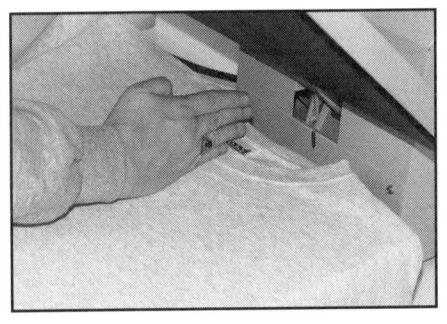

At this point, you will have the collar centered closely to the mark that you made on your heat press (or an imaginary center line). You will also have your pinched corners equally placed on either side of the bottom platen. If you have these properly centered, you shouldn't have problems with anything else.

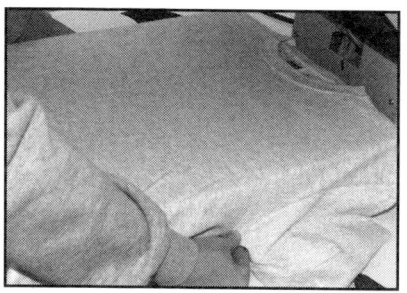

Cindy Brown » I Made That!

3. **Align Middle/Bottom**: Now you simply follow the centering process downward. Making sure that you have equal shirt overhanging each side of your platen. If your shirt is smaller than the platen, you want equal press padding showing on each side.

4. **Front Aligning Transfer**: Now that you've successfully aligned your shirt onto the press, it's time to get your transfer aligned properly on the shirt. We place (using thermal vinyl in this example) the transfer onto the front of the shirt about four fingers (or inches) below the collar, centered directly below the collar. Verify that your placement is correct, and press the transfer.

5. **Back Aligning Transfer**: Similarly to the example above, now we're ready to place a back transfer. Transfers for the backs of garments are typically placed about 5" below the collar. I also use a measurement of approximately 3" below the lower collar.

Be sure that you keep your transfers away from anything that would create a 'bump' under them. The front collar, though usually hidden under the back collar, can ruin a transfer if it creates a

B7 » Aligning the Transfer

raised area under the transfer on the back side of the shirt. Once the back transfer is properly aligned, do a visual check , and press.

6. **Voila**! Successfully aligning your shirt and transfer is not difficult at all once you know how it's done. You've just done your first successful heat transfer shirt!

FINISHED TRANSFERRED SHIRT

Your First Transfer

Standard Transfer onto White Shirt

Well, we've learned some of the basics, now it's time to really make your first transfer. I remember when I made my first transfer. The artwork was hideous (I'm not an artist). I used one of those t-shirt software programs that has clip art and text templates. It was very simple to use, but definitely not something that I would have wanted to wear out in public. Somehow though, that first shirt instantly became my favorite article of clothing.

That same day, my husband and I made about a dozen shirts. I realized after about three shirts I knew I would never wear, that it was time to figure out how to come up with some better artwork to put on the shirts. My husband on the other hand was having a blast. So, I took the kids out for some errands and left him home to make another 8 or 9 shirts. He wore them constantly and my daughter and I ended up with several new 'night shirts'.

The sheer excitement of creating your first shirts is something that will likely stay with you. I still get giggly when I create a new design or see something that I know is going to have special meaning for the customer. When I see their faces light up and I know that I had a part in that, it just makes my day. The best thing of all is that I actually get paid to make people happy!

If you're ready, let's go!

B8 » Your First Transfer

1. **Prepare the Press**: I don't want to overstate the obvious, but if you haven't tinkered with your press yet, you might not realize that it does take about 15-30 minutes to reach its full heat setting. You will need to read your paper instructions to determine the heat and time that you will need to press your shirts (or other blanks).

2. **Create & Print Artwork**: You should have already created the artwork for your first project. If you don't have something in mind already, simply scanning a photograph and printing it will also work as a good first project. See the Printing & Scanning section for tips.

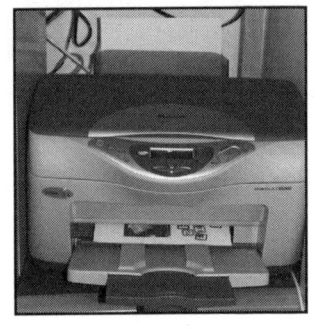

I use a CX5200 model for most of my regular sized transfers. This model has already been replaced by the CX5400, which is being replaced by the CX6400. I purchased the CX5200 only about six months ago. You can see how quickly the models change. The newer models are coming out with slots for digital camera memory cards and can print directly from the card.

I print my transfers at the 'text and image' or the 'photo' setting. We covered the printer specifics in the Printer Tutorial section. If you are skipping around as you read, you might want to refer to the Printer Tutorial section for more details.

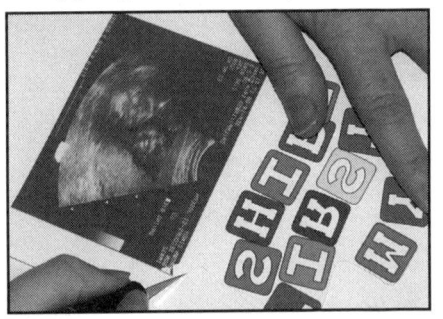

3. **Trim**: Trim around the design being careful not to touch the printed area, if possible.

Cindy Brown » I Made That!

You can use scissors or a blade to trim. I regularly use both. I find that as long as I keep a sharp blade in the knife that it is much quicker to trim (and more precise) this way than it is with scissors. However, if I am not near a surface where I can use the blade safely, I'll use a scissors.

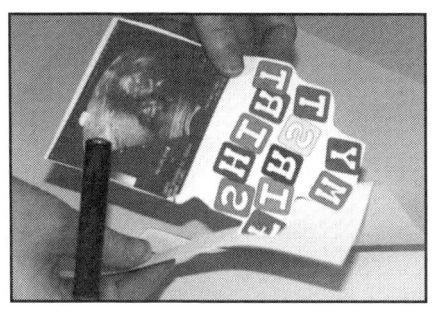

You should follow the directions for the transfer paper that you use, but most papers recommend trimming approximately 1/8" - 1/4" outside the printed area. On a white blank you can get away with trimming a much broader area than this, however, it's best to get in the habit of doing it correctly from the start.

4. **Align Blank**: It's time to align your blank (t-shirt or mousepad or whatever you're going to transfer to). We covered this in depth in the Aligning Tutorial. Please refer to that section if you need help. The project I am showing is a toddler romper. I wanted to show the aligning process for an item smaller than the press as we already showed the aligning for larger items. You can see that the outfit is placed in the center of the press which will make aligning the transfer easier.

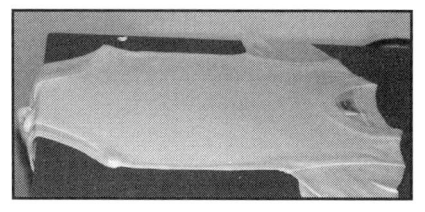

5. **Look Out**! Always be aware as you put your blanks onto the press that there might be things that can cause trouble for your transfers. In this case, the snaps at the

B8 » Your First Transfer

bottom are a potential trouble-maker. The problem is easily remedied here by simply lowering the outfit to allow the snaps to hang over the edge. If you are dealing with neck area snaps or buttons, you might want to try some other methods of placing your garment on the press.

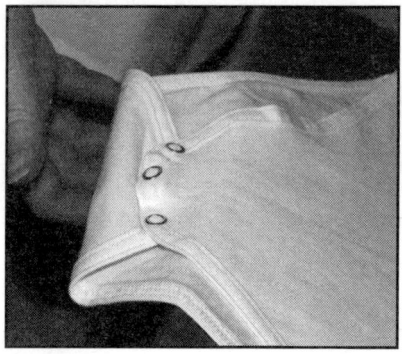

One thing that I do fairly often in cases like this is to open the garment up and place it over the bottom platen. Another simpler method is to move the problem parts just off the pressing field. If you have buttons down the center (or a zipper), simply move the entire blank over to one side or the other (usually to your left if you're pressing a pocket area transfer on the shirt's left side).

Once out of the way, just align with the straight edge of the side seam along the straight line of the heat press.

6. **Pre-Press**. This might seem like a lot of steps, but once you get used to the process, you can usually create a front and back transferred item in a minute or less. Each step is important so be sure not to skip steps until you are confident and understand why each step is necessary. The pre-press process is

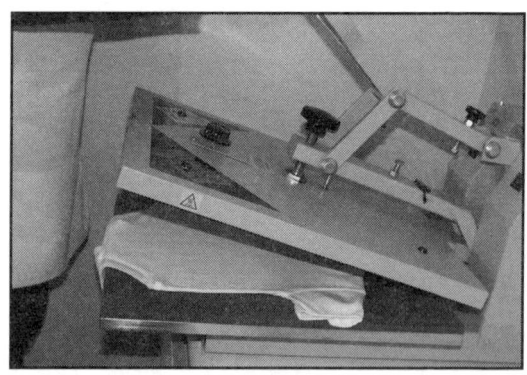

done for a couple of reasons. First, you need a flat, unwrinkled surface to work . Secondly, when these items are made, they are often treated with certain chemicals that assist in the manufacturing process. The pre-press step helps to force any humidity and chemicals out of the blank. This will help you to always have a consistent starting point that you can count on each time you press a garment.

Before putting a transfer on the garment, just lower the press handle and lock it into place for about 3-5 seconds.

7. **Align Transfer**. As we learned in the aligning section, finding your center points is an important step in making sure that your transfer will be placed in the correct location. For this particular project, we are using a graphic with text above it. It might be a little difficult to see that in the illustration because the transfer paper is placed ink side down on the garment. There is no need for heat tape in a situation like this since the baby outfit is small enough that you can easily determine if the transfer is place evenly.

8. **Press**. Now simply lower the press arm, making sure that it locks into its proper position. Refer to your transfer paper instructions for the proper pressing time. Some papers require that the instructions be followed exactly while other papers are more flexible.

You might want to experiment a little too as you get used to how the different brands work with your press. If you

B8 » Your First Transfer

are like me, once you find a good paper, you will stay with it and not want to mess with any others. I recommend that you test at least 2-3 papers before choosing the one that you want to stick with, however.

Some people might get lucky and find a good paper on the first try but I still recommend they test a couple other papers simply so they can compare the quality of their final products and know for sure that theirs is the best. It also doesn't hurt to know what some of the competition is using.

If your press has a timer, set it to the recommended time. If it doesn't, you can either purchase a digital timer or simply count (one Mississippi, two Mississippi).

9. **Peel**. The peeling step is very important. You should always peel from one corner to the opposite corner in one smooth step.

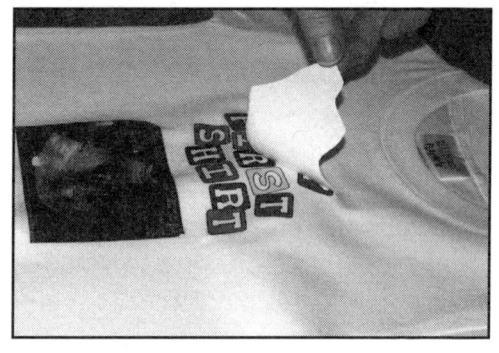

Some papers require that you peel right away while the transfer is still hot while others recommend you wait until it has cooled.

I personally do not use a cool peel paper. I've found that a hot peel produces a softer 'hand' (the stiffness of the transfer) than a cool peel although that may differ from one brand of paper to another. You may also find that the hot peel gives your transfer more of a matte finish where many of the cool-peel papers seem to leave a satin or shiny finish.

I never liked feeling like there was a painting on my shirt, so the matte finish and softer hand/feel is what I personally prefer. Others *do* like the thicker, shinier transfer. It's totally a matter of preference.

10. **Cool**. This step is a little on the obvious side as well. However, I did want to mention it. If you find yourself in a situation where you have customers waiting for your finished products, don't let them rush the process.

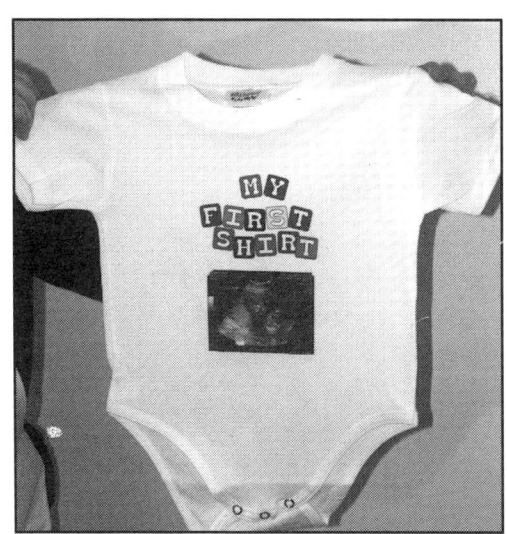

If you fold the transfer while it is still hot, you could create a crease, which isn't fatal to the transfer necessarily... but it could be. It's always a good idea to let it cool completely before folding or bagging your newly made product.

NOTE: If this were a 2-sided item, you would follow the process up to step 9, peel the first side, lay down a sheet of Teflon or other form of protective material (to protect both the newly pressed transfer as well as the bottom pad of your press). Then place the transfer on the second side (no need to pre-press again), heat for the recommended time, lift the press and peel hot as you did with the first side.

B9 » Transfers to Light Colors

Transfers to Lights

A Little Lesson Before the Project

Now we're going to transfer onto a light colored shirt. Though many papers say that they can be used only on whites that's not always true.

The paper that I use is great for whites, but also can be used successfully with many light shades as well. You just have to keep in mind that when you transfer onto colored shirts, the color of your shirt will be the lightest color you will have in your artwork. You should also be aware that the shirt color will affect the colors you print on top of it.

If, for instance, you are going to press onto a sky blue shirt, anything that is white in your artwork will be sky blue; anything that is colored in your artwork will be a combination of sky blue (from the color of the shirt) plus the colors in your artwork.

Here's a color illustration to show what I mean:

http://personalizedsupplies.com/coloredshirts.htm

As long as you remember that the inks that we use are not opaque and that there is no white ink in a typical printer, you'll quickly learn how to compensate for these limitations.

Here are a few options to help you use your normal whites /lights transfer paper for printing on colored shirts. If the design you want to use simply won't work on a colored background, even a light one, you should consider either using an opaque paper or you may need to have a screen printer so that particular job for you.

A. Create a border around the artwork, with no background color. The carrier will give slight coloring to the artwork. The border will make it appear that the slight color difference is intentional while giving a clean, professional appearance. You can see in illustration A that the colors are almost identical, but the border helps the slight shading from the paper carrier look pleasing.

B. Print a darker background than the material and leave text or graphics inside blank/white. The transfer paper will discolor the text slightly but the color that shows through will look close to the color of the shirt. Trim to the very edge of the border.

C. Without a background and/or border, the carrier (the part the transfer leaves behind) will look something like the third illustration below. It will always show when pressed on anything other than white and some very light materials and will usually make your shirt look very unprofessional.

Basically, all you won't be able to do is make any part of your design white or lighter than the color of the shirt (unless you use an opaque paper).

Now that we understand some of the basics about working with a "normal" non-opaque transfer paper for whites/lights when printing on colored shirts, let's try a normal t-shirt transfer onto an ash gray shirt.

There are a few gray shades that are common. Ash gray is probably the lightest gray you will normally find and is quite nice to work with using the whites/lights transfer paper as long as you keep in mind the problems that can occur when using whites/lights paper on anything other than a white shirt.

B9 » Transfers to Light Colors

There are some other shades of gray (Heather and Athletic Gray) that might work as well. These are about the darkest colors that you'll probably be able to work with using a whites/lights transfer paper.

As far as the other colors, you will find that there are so many shades and brands that it is impossible to give an exact answer as to whether a particular one will be an acceptable shade to work without going to an opaque paper.

My best advice is ask others in the industry what kind of results they have had with these colors. Of course, experience is the best teacher. If you can, you may want to just try a few of them out for yourself.

Project:

Transfer Onto a Light to Medium Colored Shirt

1. **Align the Shirt**: Using the method I prefer, pinch the shoulder seams and center over the press. Then align the side of the shirt along the edge of your transfer press.

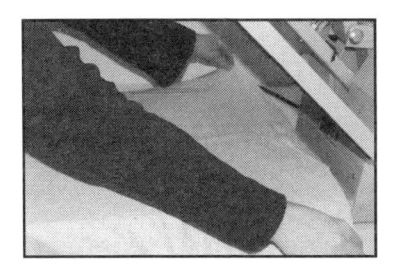

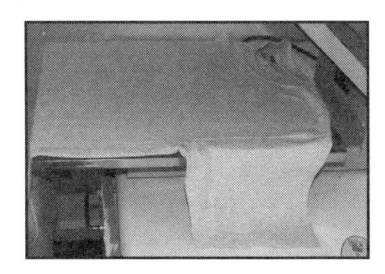

2. **Trim the Artwork**: Because this transfer will be going onto a colored shirt, it is vital that you trim very close to the edge of the artwork. Leaving excess white areas on the outside of the artwork will result in part of the carrier showing The carrier is the material that holds the inks onto the shirt.

Either scissors or a sharp blade knife can be used to trim. I found that once you have practiced awhile, the knife is much faster.

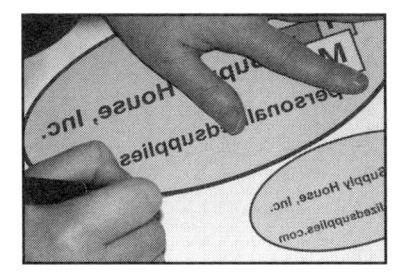

B9 » Transfers to Light Colors

3. **Place the Transfer**: It's a good idea to remember your measurements (found in the Aligning Tutorial) when placing your transfer.

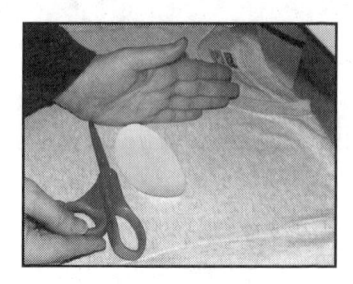

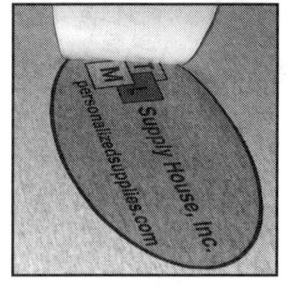

4. **Heat & Peel**: As you would any ordinary transfer, cook the transfer on the shirt for an appropriate period of time and peel according to the instructions.

Examples of Transfers On Ash Gray Shirt

Clear Background With Black Border

Peach Background as Shown in Tutorial Above

Opaque Transfer to *Darks*

Project: Black Long-Sleeved Knit

Opaque material is a specialty paper for doing digital transfers onto medium to dark materials. The washability and life expectancy of an opaque transfer is typically not nearly as long as one done with a quality whites or lights transfer paper.

I suggest that you sample many brands of opaque paper prior to choosing one particular opaque paper as some are very different in quality. Follow the directions for opaque materials very carefully.

Opaque transfers are great for the customer who has a realistic expectation of the lifetime of a shirt made with opaque material.

Here we go!

1. **Align and Clean:** Align your shirt on the press. I use a lint roller brush to clean off any visible lint from the blank garment.

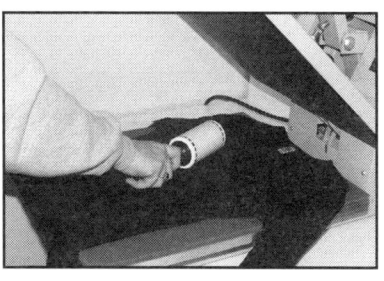

2. **Pre-Press:** Pre-Press your shirt or other dark item for about 3-5 seconds. This helps get rid of any humidity in the material as well as any possible chemicals that might be in the material from the factory.

3. **Trim Transfer:** It is vital when working with an opaque paper that you trim the design

B10 » Opaque Transfer to Darks

all the way to the edge. Otherwise, the white of the carrier will show up around the transfer.

Opaque transfer paper is a thin paper with a plastic-like feel. It is essentially a non-sticky material that you melt onto the blank. Because it is held onto the shirt entirely through the pressing process, make sure you get the transfer fully and firmly attached.

4. **Peel**: Now is the time to peel the paper backing off the front part that you have printed onto. These papers can often be fragile and can rip easily as you peel. Use caution to avoid rips. A rip will usually mean the end of that transfer.

Another suggestion for dealing with opaque material is to round off edges and avoid small, pointed designs like the plague because when you wash the blank, over time (sometimes the first wash, sometimes several washes later), these materials have been known to start to peel away from the shirts.

We don't want to see that happen so it's usually best to create a background (like above image) for an opaque transfer so that the design can be attractive, but will not have fragile areas that would be more prone coming loose and ruining the shirt.

5. **Place:** Place opaque material onto the blank where you would like it to be transferred.

6. **Cover:** Cover the opaque material with a siliconized sheet (typically included with the the opaque material).

7. **Cook**: Cook the material according to the instructions that come with the opaque paper. Since so many are different, always read the instructions.

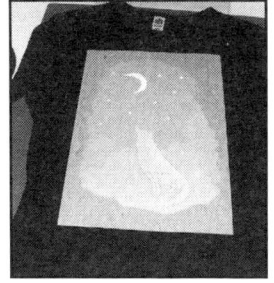

8. **Rub & Set**: As soon as you lift the heat platen from the shirt, take a thick item (such as a blank mousepad) and rub completely over the transfer. Since this is a film of sorts, and is being slightly melted to make it adhere to the shirt, you should be sure that there are no air pockets or spots where uneven temperatures might cause problems with the transfer.

Typically, I rub for about 3-5 seconds until the transfer has had a chance to start to cool down.

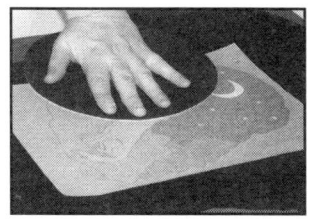

If you've begun to peel before rubbing the transfer, just stop. Rub and set the transfer, and then begin the peeling process again.

9. **Peel**: You're almost done. Peel slowly and steadily from corner to corner of the siliconized paper.

B10 » Opaque Transfer to Darks

10. **Re-Press**: This last stage is optional with some papers. Some people like to re-press using a sheet of Teflon to give it a glossier look. I personally prefer the matte finish that it gets when I press the first time with the siliconized paper. If you do re-press the blank, make sure that you place the siliconized sheet or a Teflon® sheet over the new transfer to protect it.

There you have it – your finished opaque material transfer. Make sure that you do intensive washing tests on any opaque materials that you purchase so that you can give your customers an estimate of how long their new shirt will last. Also, if you find specific washing methods (such as turning inside out) that help keep the garment from cracking or fading, share that with your customers as well.

Congratulations! You've made it through the Darks tutorial.

Thermal Vinyl on Colored Materials

Project: Zippered Jacket

In this lesson, we will learn how to apply thermal vinyl on a dark material by creating a personalized zippered jacket with a single color, thermal vinyl, large back print.

By this point, I am going to assume that you've already learned the basics of heat transfer application. If you haven't, you might want to review section B8, standard first transfer, to fill in any possible gaps.

1. **Design your artwork**: You should use vector art for designs that will be cut with a cutter/plotter. We will print a zippered jacket with a large back print and a smaller pocket area print.

Customers will often want personalized text and sometimes will use clip art as well, but text is most commonly used with thermal vinyl.

2. **Send artwork to plotter**: This is done differently from plotter to plotter. Please consult the plotter owner's manual for detailed instructions.

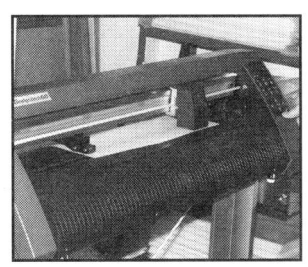

24" plotter with stand

B11 » Thermal Vinyl on Colored Materials

3. **Cut vinyl off the plotter:** Cut the thermal vinyl off the roll. This material is not terribly expensive, but it isn't cheap either. You should use it wisely.

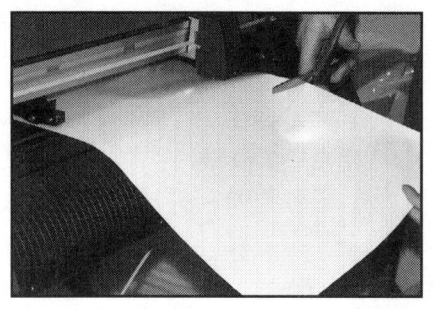

Using scissors, cut the vinyl off the roll.

4. **Begin weeding**: This is simply the process of removing and discarding excess material from the desired artwork.

5. **Fine weeding**: You will also need to make sure that you remove the inner areas of your graphics and text. These are the insides of the 'O' for example. Make sure to get them out now because after you press the artwork, it's too late!

6. **Align the garment**: Aligning your garment properly is probably one of the most important things to do. After a few mistakes though, you will become a pro. I recommend finding a middle point on your heat press. Mark it with a marker for future reference. Find your center of your garment as well, and voila!

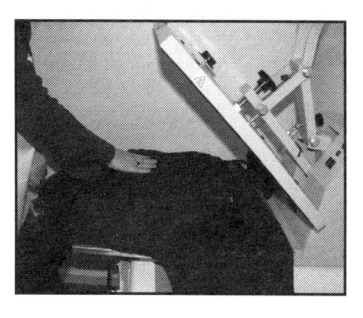

7. **Pre-Press garment**: Lower the press and pre-press the garment for approximately 3-6 seconds.

8. **Align the thermal vinyl**: Equally important as aligning your garment is aligning your vinyl. Where the excess vinyl was removed, you will notice that it is sticky. This slight stickiness helps you align and keep your material in place.

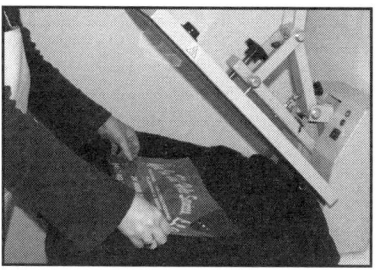

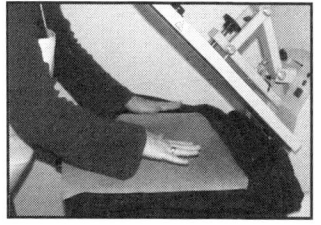

9. **Cover with Teflon® or similar material**: This is to protect the press as well as to act as a buffer for the vinyl.

B11 » Thermal Vinyl on Colored Materials

10. **Heat**: The material I use is heated for 20 seconds at 350°F using heavy pressure. Make sure that you check the instructions for the material you use.

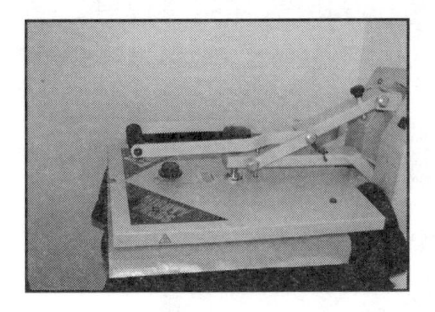

11. **Lift and Rub**: This is an important step. When the time has elapsed, take a padded item (I use a blank mousepad) and rub it carefully along the entire surface of the vinyl (with the film still attached). This helps cool your project preparing it for the peeling process. More importantly it helps to set the vinyl to the garment.

A towel or other insulated item could work instead of a mousepad blank, if you like.

12. **Peel:** Peel the film away from the vinyl. Some materials require cool peel while others need warm.

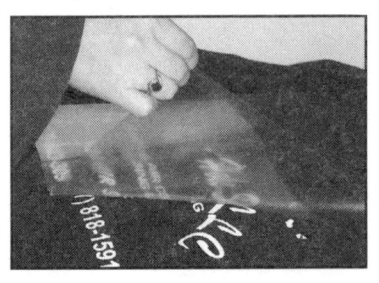

13. **Replace Teflon® and Re-Press**: This is an optional step for many but I perform this step every single time. It helps ensure there is solid adhesion of the material to the garment. I do this for an additional 6-10 seconds.

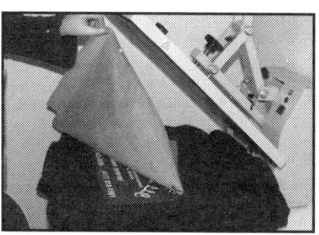

14. **Remove, Cool**: That's it. You're finished! Make sure to let the vinyl material cool completely prior to folding to avoid creasing and/or sticking.

Transfers to Accessories

Project: Tote Bag

Tote bags have never been a product that I found much use for until I began working in this industry. I guess I never was a tote bag 'type' (whatever that is).

When I began doing transfers though, I realized that totes can be pretty darn fun. While they may not be huge sellers, you might find that tote bags can be a great product that you can market to businesses as a promotional giveaway item printed with company information.

The totes that I use almost exclusively now I found at a wholesale supplier on the Internet. They are white with colored handles and even have a little outside pocket (handy for cell phones). These are actually attractive enough that people truly enjoy carrying them around.

One word of caution, always wipe your heat press down with a blank mousepad or towel after pressing onto these colored totes. The tote bags often leave a faint residue behind that can show up on (and ruin) the next item you press.

It only takes one or two ruined items to help you remember to wipe your press down. Hopefully, by reading this book, you won't ruin as many blanks as I did which would basically have paid for your book!

If you're ready, let's make a tote bag like the one on the cover of this book. This is a very popular format for totes in our store. Another one is putting 'Grandma's Little Angels' in text and a mini angel on a cloud with a name for each of their grandkids.

1. **Create, Print, & Trim Artwork**: We have already covered this thoroughly by now.

2. **Align Tote**: With this particular tote bag, it has a plastic-like interior. If you simply place it on the press you will probably find that the insides stick together (ruining it). For this reason, I open the tote and put one side above the press and the other side below the press.

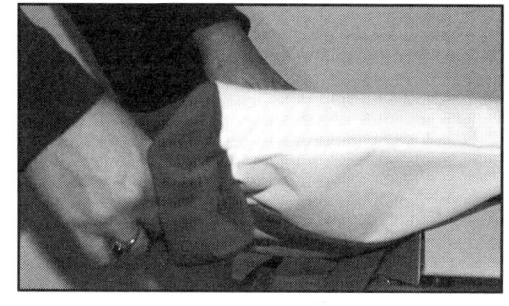

If your press is bigger than a 16x20, this will not work since it's very snug on my 16x20 with these particular tote bags (perfect for my press).

The key to a successful print on a tote like this is that you have to lay it very smoothly so that the transfer sits flat on the surface. Keeping the puckers/wrinkles out is crucial for a successful transfer.

3. **Align Transfer**: We have trimmed to a reasonable distance around the transfer. This is being transferred onto a white surface, so trimming right up to the edge isn't really vital.

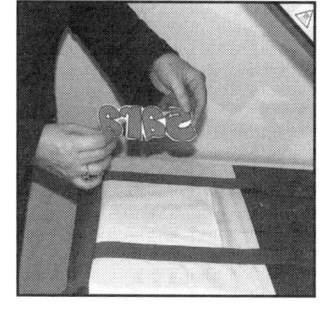

In most totes that are all one color and have shoulder straps that are also the same material and color, you will not have to worry about separating the sides of the tote since most of them are made of a canvas-type material and the insides won't stick together when pressed.

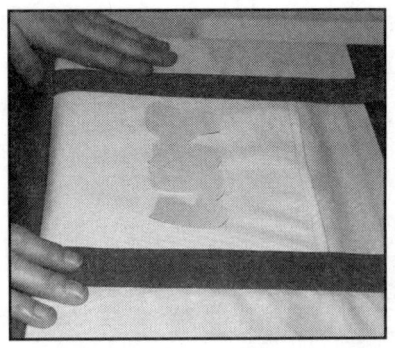

B12 » Transfers to Accessories

4. **Cover & Protect:** I use a sheet of Teflon to cover the handles of the tote bags (only on this type, not the natural colored fabric totes). I do this because, like the insides, the heat from the press will begin to melt the handles otherwise.

It doesn't do any sort of damage to them in the brief time that we actually press the tote (approximately 14 seconds). However, the colors can sometimes bleed onto the heat press. The Teflon helps to protect the press from the residue that would be picked up from the handles as well as protecting the handles from excessive heat.

5. **Cook & Peel**: The 'cook' time and temperature is typically not any different than your normal shirt transfers. Peel the transfer paper according to instructions on the package and you should have a great personalized tote bag that you and many others would be proud to have over their shoulders.

« 134 »

There are many other accessories that you can transfer to. The main determining factor will be if the item is white or has a white area on it. The next and also very important question you need to ask is whether the product can tolerate the heat of approximately 350°F. If your answer to both of these questions is yes, you can probably transfer onto it successfully.

Here is a brief list of items that will make good personalized products. There are many others that you might find and want to experiment with. Just use common sense when you come up with new ideas and you could discover the next great craze!

APRONS

BABY BIBS

BANDANNAS

CAN COOLIES

CHECKBOOK COVERS

KITCHEN TOWELS

MEMO CUBES

MOUSE PADS

PET APPAREL

PET ACCESSORIES

POT HOLDERS (NON-HEAT SIDE)

PURSES

PUZZLES

SPORTS TOWELS

TOTE BAGS

B13» Transfers Onto Other Blanks

Transfers Onto Other Blanks

Project: Ball Cap

Now we will take a look at doing transfers onto other items. The primary purpose for this is to show the method of aligning and so forth since we've already covered the the actual process of performing the transfer.

First we'll start with a ball cap. I thought I would do the toughest project possible. With this in mind, I am going to do a baby ball cap!

The reason this is a difficult project is because cap presses usually have more than one size heat platen. They usually include a standard and a low profile platen. Keep this in mind when you order your ball caps. If your cap press matches the ball caps, it will make the job much simpler.

They can still be done if your press is larger than your cap, but I sure wouldn't recommend trying to do a large cap on a low profile platen for obvious reasons.

1. **Align**: As you can see in the photo, the ball cap is considerably smaller than the mold that the cap goes around. This isn't an ideal situation by any means, and I recommend using the right size of cap platen, but

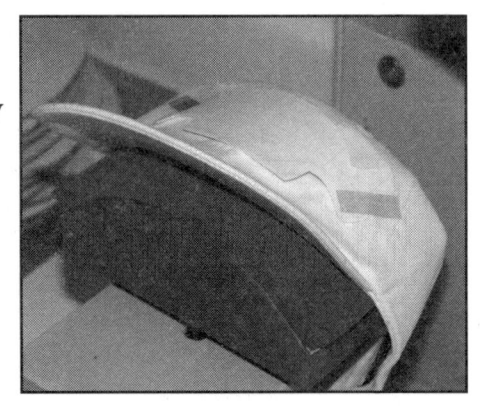

it can still be pressed with successful results almost every time. Would it be simpler if we had the right sized platen? Without a doubt, yes. Is it possible to do a large cap transfer onto a low profile press? I have never attempted it, but logic says no.

If the cap is larger than the press, you will have transfer material hanging over the actual heatable area. While some might say (and even try with limited success) that you can press part of the cap, then move it to try to press the other part, I haven't found that to be a consistently reliable method.

On this project, we are reasonably safe doing a smaller hat on a larger pressing area. Be aware that when we close the press on the cap, the pressure of the press will quite likely crease the bill of the cap when it is also caught in the press due to the size mismatch.

2. **Heat Tape**: This is a great time to use your heat tape. Aligning the transfer on a curved item can be a little tougher to do. To clarify, it's not tough to place the transfer, but to keep it in place. Make sure that you don't try this with regular tape.

3. **Press & Peel**: As you normally would with any transfer, press the cap and peel the transfer paper.

B13» Transfers Onto Other Blanks

Project: Apron

Putting transfers on most apron materials is quite simple. In fact, other than placement, there is very little difference between an apron and a t-shirt. The materials might be different depending on where the apron is purchased.

You also want to be sure you don't purchase an apron that is made with Teflon®. While the idea for making aprons with Teflon® is a good one (to keep things from sticking), it makes things pretty difficult when we *want* to get something to stick to it.

At many wholesale suppliers (as well as your local hobby stores), you should be able to easily find several styles of aprons that will meet your needs.

1. **Align**: The biggest factor in aligning a transfer on an apron is going to be the size of your transfer. If you are doing a company logo or a short line of text, the spot on the apron pictured here is a great location for it.

However, if you want to use a graphic and/or text that is considerably larger, I would align the top of your transfer about 4"-5" from the top seam.

Some aprons are very long while some barely cover the lap area. There are many to choose from to suit the needs of each job you may get.

(Psst... an apron is a nice protector for your own clothes as you work with your inks and other messy things.)

Signs

Project: Auto Magnetics

If you have (or plan to have) the plotter for making thermal vinyl transfers, it is a logical addition to add a few sign options to your product line.

As I mentioned before, I'd leave the big sign jobs to the sign companies. But, as a former owner and employee of a couple of sign shops, I've found that smaller signs are hardly worth the time for the big sign shops.

If you don't have a local shop that offers 24-hour processing for banners and signs, it might be a great service that you can offer in your area.

When vinyl signs became widely used and replaced the sign painters who actually hand painted the lettering onto signs and autos, it opened a door to many of us with computer graphics skills, but who couldn't paint a sign to save our lives (that's me).

There is no replacement for a true sign painter. I was married to one (ok, I replaced him, but that's not the point). He and his brother learned the trade from their father who was also a sign painter. A true sign painter is a gifted artist and can create absolute wonders.

Unless you already have these very special skills, I suggest you don't try to get into that market. What we can do and do well, is great auto magnetics, banners, yard signs and more. Granted these are lower priced signs but, if you do them well, your reputation for creating quality products quickly will travel. This can be a great addition to your transfers business. If you're ready, we're

B14 » Signs – Car Magnetics

going to make a 12" x 24" set of magnetics for a new pet grooming business.

1. **Create Artwork**: As you gain experience in creating custom graphics, you will find creating artwork for signs is much the same. The main difference is that you'll be working with single colors rather than digital output.

One big difference is that for most plotters, you create your text and artwork without color. When you have created the artwork the way you envision it completed, simply 'select all' and change the color to white for everything.

While you still have all the objects selected, add a hairline outline to everything. If you want multiple colors on the same project blank (in this case, we're doing car magnetics and only doing one color), simply divide the objects in sections so that you have all the colors grouped to cut at the same time. You'll align them on the blank later.

2. **Send Artwork to Plotter**: Each plotter will probably have a different method for sending the artwork. See your user manual for this information.

When you send artwork to the plotter for a thermal vinyl transfer, you cut in reverse. When doing a regular sign, you do not cut in reverse (also called 'mirror'). If you can remember which gets cut as a mirror image and which doesn't, you'll soon be able to simply send the artwork without even thinking about it.

3. **Prepare Magnetic Material**: More than likely you will be purchasing your magnetic material on a roll so that you can cut it to suit each individual customer.

When I cut the magnetic material, I unroll it onto a flat, hard surface. Make sure that the surface is clean because the magnetic material can be damaged by debris that might be on your work area.

You will always want to use a straight edge to cut the material. Being even a little bit off of your measurements can degrade the appearance of the finished product. Cut from the back side (the black) in a smooth single cut if at all possible.

4. **Separate**: If your blade did not go through completely, you can fold the material back onto itself to create a break in the black side. Once you have done this, reverse your fold and apply gentle pressure to create a break in the white side.

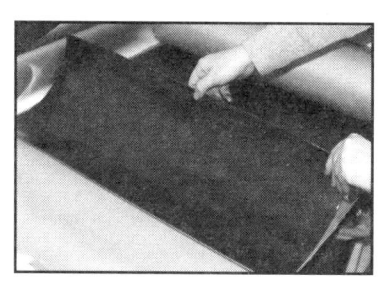

5. **Clean Material**: It is always a good idea to clean your material before applying vinyl. Some might skip this step and still be successful at times but I recommend always cleaning to avoid the potential for poor results.

6: **A Crutch**. While some might think of my next sug-

B14 » Signs – Car Magnetics

gestion as a crutch, I think that using a spray such as Rapid Tac is a wise and precautionary measure. Often called a wet procedure, a spray like this gives the user time to 'float' (or reposition) the vinyl without risk of ruining it which is what would happen if you were to place it slightly off center the without the Rapid Tac.

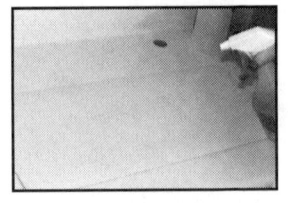

It works as a residue-free cleaner as well as adhesive stimulant. Using this product or another one like it has simplified the process and all but eliminated failed attempts for me in every single sign I have made with it.

Now that you know what it is, simply spray it across the entire surface of the magnetic material. You want it to be wet enough that the vinyl will not stick to the magnetic material when you begin to place it.

7. **Weed**: As we learned in the thermal vinyl tutorial, it's time to weed the excess away now.

8. **Apply Tape**: You should use a product called application tape. It is available in assorted widths. I keep several widths so that I won't have to waste the excess. However, one size will work fine if you don't think you'll use it often enough to justify buying more than one.

There are several methods you can use to apply this to your weeded vinyl. I have found that on the signs I typically make, since they are generally small, I can simply pull it off the roll, then softly apply pressure to the tape starting at one side as it adheres to the vinyl.

9. **Squeegee**: Take your squeegee (who came up with that name?) and, in short strokes, apply pressure in a painting-like motion. This makes the vinyl stick to your application tape more than it will stick to the paper beneath the vinyl.

10. **Peel Paper**: Peel the paper away from the vinyl and application tape. If you notice any of it sticking to the paper instead of the tape, stop and squeegee again.

Depending on the size of the piece you are working with, you might want to peel after you have placed your vinyl onto the blank. If it is small enough to be easily handled, you can peel it entirely.

11. **Apply to Magnetic**: Now, you simply apply the vinyl to the magnetic material. You should first take some measurements to determine where your center point is so that you can align your vinyl properly.

If you are using a spray, you can set the vinyl down and, if you find that your measurements aren't correct, you can simply lift it up and replace it correctly.

After you have it placed properly and while the tape is still over it, squeegee the vinyl onto the magnetic material. Take special care at this point to be certain that you don't have air bubbles between the magnetic material and the vinyl. If you see bubbles, squeegee them out carefully.

B14 » Signs – Car Magnetics

12. **Re-spray**: Some people skip this step. I have found that it usually helps do it. After vinyl is adhered to the magnetic material, spray your surface again. This helps loosen the application tape from your vinyl. It will still peel away without re-spraying, it just might not be as smooth or as easy.

13. **Peel Tape**: You're ready to peel the application tape away from the magnetic material now. If you did the previous step, the tape will come up very easily. If you didn't, you may find some resistance when the tape pulls away from the magnetic. Either is normal shouldn't be a problem.

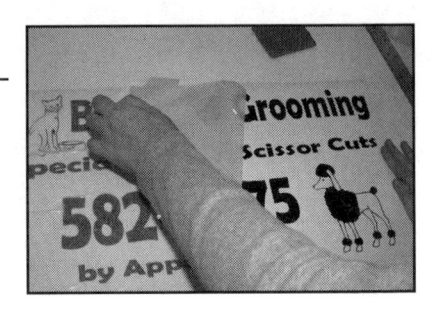

14. **Completed Item**: And there you have it. A finished car magnetic. Most people don't buy one magnetic, but typically buy them in pairs. Make sure that they look as close to identical as possible.

Refiller's Guide

Refilling – Is it for you?

Some prefer to buy ink in small bulk containers of 2 or 4 ounce sizes and refill the cartridges as they begin to run out of ink. This used to be a very popular method of saving money (by not having to continually repurchase cartridges).

When the most of the printer models began to have small chips added to the printer cartridges, refilling became much more difficult. These little chips were created to help the end user know how much ink was remaining in their cartridge. This is very handy. But for the people who refill their carts, it was like having a wrench thrown into the works, so to speak.

When people ask me if they can or should refill their own cartridges for a printer that uses chipped carts, I almost always recommend against it. It has simply become too frustrating.

Refilling used to be tough when you were first learning how to do it. Now it has become darn near impossible. You might have heard the stories about friends or co-workers who tried to use one of those universal ink kits from a discount store and made such a mess that they ended up going back for pre-filled OEM cartridges swearing to never try that again.

Refilling is definitely not for everyone. If you have a troubleshooting mind and are up for some possible (or probable) hassles, refilling might still work for you.

I don't want to poison your mind against refilling. For

some people it is an excellent method to save some money off the costs of buying pre-filled ink cartridges.

I would like you to know, however, that the success rate for refilling the chipped cartridges is far lower than it used to be. As a former refiller who actually *enjoyed* refilling, I will no longer refill a cartridge unless I'm facing some sort of emergency. They have just become too difficult to deal with on a consistent basis.

I am going to give some very basic refilling information and techniques for those who would at least like to learn the process in order to make up their own mind.

Be aware that this book is nowhere near long enough to include a full troubleshooting guide for refilling. Feel free to visit the *I Made That! forum* online with any specific questions you might have. Here's the URL again:

http://press2success.com/imadethat/

Project: Filling New Cartridges

We will start this tutorial with a relatively simple method of filling new, virgin cartridges. This method can be used only once. If you tried to use this method a second time, the step where you create a vacuum in the cartridge would draw out the remaining ink in the cartridge rather than drawing out just the air.

Compared to purchasing pre-filled cartridges, it is still slightly less expensive to purchase empty cartridges and bulk inks even if you are going to only fill them one time.

Read on for the brief process that it takes to fill unused cartridges using the *vacuum method*.

Cindy Brown » I Made That!

1. **Set up your area**: I strongly recommend working over a sink, counter top or other area that can be protected from ink splatters and spills. If you goof and you weren't well enough protected, you'll want your work area to be one that can be easily cleaned up. Most quality pigmented inks are highly likely to stain.

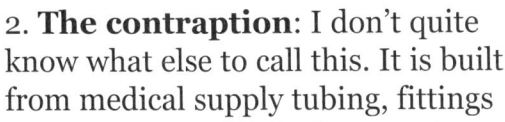

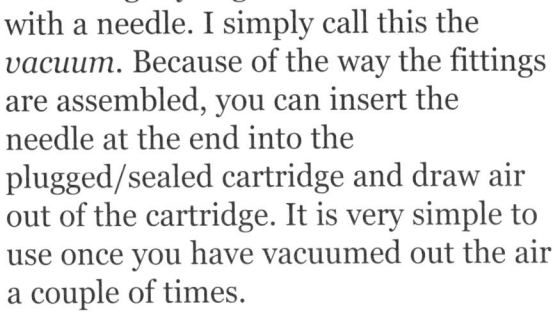

2. **The contraption**: I don't quite know what else to call this. It is built from medical supply tubing, fittings and a large syringe with a needle. I simply call this the *vacuum*. Because of the way the fittings are assembled, you can insert the needle at the end into the plugged/sealed cartridge and draw air out of the cartridge. It is very simple to use once you have vacuumed out the air a couple of times.

3. **Insert Plug, Insert Needle**: Simply put the little rubber plugs that come with your cartridges into the fill holes to seal the cartridge. Then insert the needle into the cartridge by gently pushing it through the rubber plug.

This might take a little bit of practice to get the needle in without pushing the plug inside the cartridge. You can try to hold the plug with one finger while inserting and removing the syringe from the plug.

4. **Vacuum Air Out**: While the needle is inserted in the cartridge through the plug, use your syringe to pull out

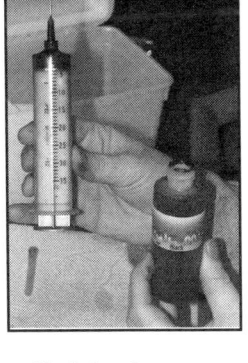

B15 » Refilling – Is it For You?

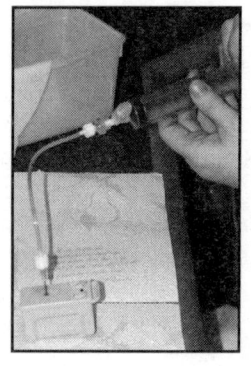

the air inside the cartridge. After you pull the syringe outward, stop and push the plunger back into the syringe. You will hear air escaping through your fittings assembly as you push it back into the syringe. Do this one or two times to perform the vacuum process.

5. **Fill Syringe**: Make certain that you know what the cartridge capacity is for the cartridges that your model uses. You can find a chart for capacities of many cartridges at

http://personalizedsupplies.com/cartridgecapacitylist.htm

Draw the ink from your bottle into the syringe. Fill the syringe to an amount that is equal to or less than the cartridge capacity for your model. This helps avoid overfilling your cartridges. In printers, more is not necessarily better. It can cause ink to leak into your printer.

6. **Insert Needle, Fill Cartridge**: Now, simply insert the needle into the cartridge through the plug. This should be as smooth an insertion as possible to avoid excess movement of the plug which could allow air back in to the cartridge. Air that gets back into the cartridge keeps the ink that should be drawn in from being pulled in.

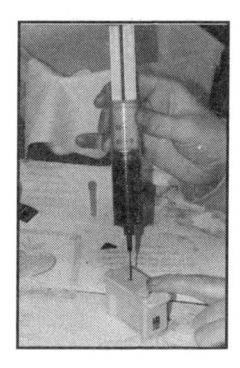

You will notice when you insert the needle that the ink is automatically drawn from the syringe into the cartridge. This is a sign that your fill is performing successfully.

7. **Release Pressure**: Take a wet wipe or a paper towel at this point and cover the chambers of the cartridges.

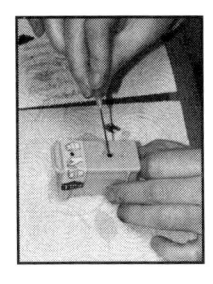

You will need to use a needle or pushpin to poke into the rubber plugs to remove them from the holes.

When you do this, you will probably notice a sound of the vacuum being released. This is good.

8. **Seal**: Once there is no longer a vacuum or pressure inside the chambers, simply replace the rubber plugs.

9. **Thump**: I know this sounds crazy, but I typically use a wrist rest (pictured) as a firm but padded material to thump the newly filled cartridges on. Of course, you want to be certain that your cartridge openings are all fully sealed and you might even want to put the cartridge inside a sandwich bag or something for extra protection from possible ink splatters.

Once completely sealed and protected, I take the cartridge in one hand and thump it firmly onto the wrist rest. I usually hit it on the bottom of the cartridge, avoiding completely the chip area of the cartridge. After about five good whacks, set it aside.

The reason for doing this is to shake out any larger pockets of air in the cartridge. Doing this will create many more mini bubbles. Make sure that you do not attempt to install and print immediately at this point. You will almost certainly have poor results if you rush it. Wait a few hours for the bubbles to dissipate before installing and using your newly filled carts.

B15 » Refilling – Is it For You?

Project: Refilling Cartridges

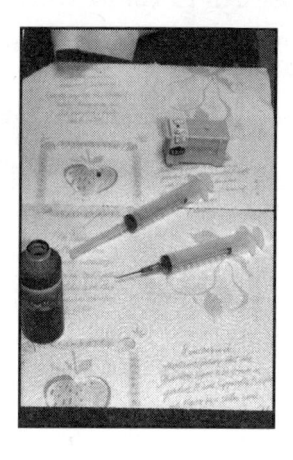

Newspaper
Baby wipes
Syringes
Needles
Tape
A pry tool (a pushpin or needle works great)
Steady hands and/or nerves (optional)

With chipped printers, the chips in the cartridges will need to be reset to make your printer think that they are brand new cartridges. A chip reprogrammer is available from many online vendors for about $20. These are not guaranteed to work on all models nor are they guaranteed to work on non OEM chips. I recommend that you investigate these little tools before you decide for sure if refilling is something you want to pursue.

The process of refilling is actually very simple but the setup is important and you will need to be prepared. You are likely to have some dripping but, if you are organized and ready for it, refilling can be a very simple, cost-saving process.

If you can, it's wise to place some newspaper on your work area. I also suggest baby wipes to help you out in case of any spills or dripping. Barely damp paper towels will also work if you don't have baby wipes.

1. **Assemble Supplies**: Put a needle on the end of each

of your syringes. Leave needle covers on whenever they're not in use. I suggest marking each syringe in some way so you'll know which color goes in each syringe. If you wash them well enough, it won't matter but I figure why take a chance of mixing the inks at all?

2. **Prepare Cartridges**: If you are starting with pre-filled cartridges, there should be a label on the top of the cartridge. It's time to take it off. Completely remove this label to expose two sets of holes on the top of the cartridge. The top holes are smaller, and called the vent holes (these are under the yellow tape when the cartridge is new).

The holes in the middle are the ones that each hold a plug. These are larger and located in the middle of the top side of the cartridge. Both the vent hole and the fill holes go to the same location inside the cartridge, but in order to not damage the cartridge, you should avoid filling through the vent holes.

3. **Seal**: Tape all openings, especially the bottom holes, so that only one opening at a time will be exposed. Many people use an electric tape for the bottom holes and, rather than removing them when you are finished refilling, they simply puncture the electric tape as if it were a new set of cartridges.

Your cartridges probably come with small plugs that go into the fill holes. There is no need to tape over these as long as they remain plugged. Best practice is to only remove one plug at a time right before refilling that chamber and immediately re-plug it when you're done.

4. **Getting Started**: Open the color that you want to fill first. I suggest doing only one color at a time to avoid

B15 » Refilling – Is it For You?

getting one color ink into another ink compartment.

Hint: If you have an OEM ink cartridge handy, place the one you are going to fill beside it. Look at the locations of each color and mark the empty cartridge with a reminder such as M=magenta, Y=yellow, C=cyan so that you will not accidentally put the incorrect ink into the tank. If, for some reason, you HAVE put the wrong color into any chamber, there is no salvaging the cartridge. Unfortunately, it's time to buy another set.

5. **Cartridge Capacity**: Find out what the cartridge capacity is for your printer model. It is important that you have an accurate fill in your cartridges so that the ink monitor in the printer will be accurate. You can find a chart for capacities of many cartridges at http://personalizedsupplies.com/cartridgecapacitylist.htm

6. **Fill Syringe**: Draw into your syringe in equal increments (possibly 5 or 10 ml at a time) the ink color you want to start with.

Since each printer cartridge usually will have a different capacity, you might want to use an amount that will help you remember exactly how much you have filled.

Air pockets can keep you from getting your cartridge to full capacity. AIR is your worst enemy when filling or refilling cartridges.

7. **Begin Fill**: Slowly and carefully, insert the needle into the fill hole for the proper color. Place it fairly deeply into the cartridge. Be careful not to force the needle as it could damage the cartridge.

8. **Fill**: Squeeze the ink gradually into the cartridge, being careful not to fill too quickly so that it overflows or introduces more air than is already inside the cartridge. If it does overflow, simply take a barely damp wet wipe or paper towel and blot it off.

9. **Replace Plug**: When finished with each color, place a rubber stopper or tape over the hole you just filled and make certain that it is airtight.

10. **Continue**: Continue to fill the other colors and the black tanks in the same manner. One at a time, replacing tape as necessary.

11. **Thump**: I know this sounds crazy, but I typically use a wrist rest (pictured) as a firm but padded material to thump the newly filled cartridges on. Of course, you want to be certain that your cartridge openings are all fully sealed and you might even want to put the cartridge inside a sandwich bag or something for extra protection from possible ink splatters.

Once completely sealed and protected, I take the cartridge in one hand and thump it firmly onto the wrist rest. I usually hit it on the bottom of the cartridge, completely avoiding the chip area of the cartridge. After about five good whacks, set it aside.

The reason for doing this is to shake out any larger pockets of air in the cartridge. However, this creates many more mini bubbles. Make sure that you do not attempt to install and print immediately at this point. You will almost certainly have poor results if you rush it.

B15 » Refilling – Is it For You?

12. **Wait**: Let cartridges sit for at least 30-60 minutes before putting them into your printer.

It is common for there to be ink leaking from the bottom for several minutes after you remove the bottom tape (Only if this is a refill. A first time fill will not have the holes punctured yet).

Hint: I suggest that you do not set them on anything absorbent such as paper towels that would actually draw the ink out of the cartridge. If you choose to, many people have experimented with leaving the tape on the bottom and treating it like a new cartridge (puncturing the tape when installing as mentioned above).

I have not personally done this while I was refilling, but they tell me that it works well. Some people use a good quality black electric tape and simply remove it and replace it with a new strip with each refill. You might also consider trying heat tape for this.

13. **Install Cartridges**: Place the cartridges back into the printer. You should wait a minimum of 3-6 hours (but I suggest waiting overnight to let the cartridges fully re-stabilize) before trying to print or prime the cartridges. You'll have less headaches when it's time to fully print/prime again.

14. **Prime**: You will now need to prime your cartridges/printer. You can print color bars or other colorful graphics to get the inks to flow correctly. You will also likely need to perform a print head cleaning followed by one or more test pages to make sure the bars are all printing.

You might need to raise the DPI setting temporarily if you get banding when you print now. You can usually reduce the DPI back to 720 within a few pages.

15. **Clean Up**: Make certain that you have washed all tools completely, and store them in a safe place until the next use.

Please see the Epson site for any technical issues with your printer regarding the print head cleanings. I am not an Epson tech nor am I familiar with all the Epson models. The manufacturer is always the best resource for accurate information on repairs and technical information.

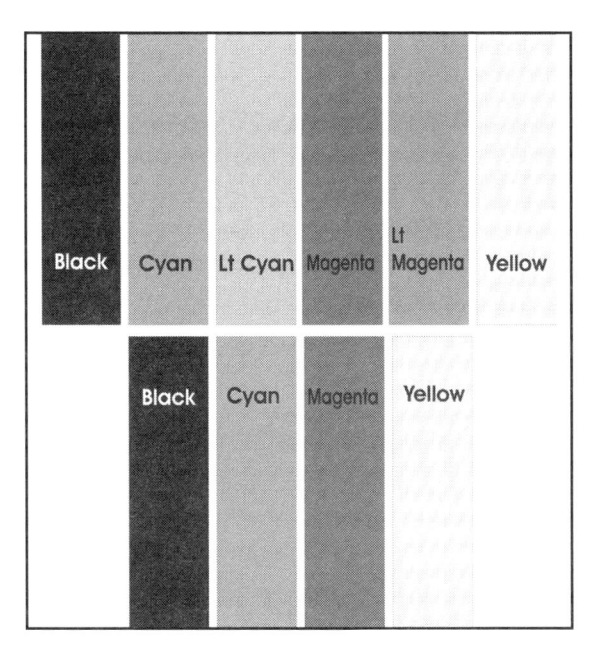

Ink order for six- and four-color models is shown here.

B15 » Refilling – Is it For You?

Bulk Units

There is another option available to those who want to save money and still use a high quality ink. A bulk unit, made of an assortment of medical supplies is a great tool to add to your system.

There is a growing list of vendors for these units. I have included the URLs of several in the supplies directory at the back of the book. I do suggest that you shop carefully for your bulk unit if you choose to add one. The failure ratio for these units can be fairly high if not very carefully assembled and installed.

When manufactured, installed, and used properly, these are wonderful to use. You can cut your cost per print from approximately $1 +/- a page to around $.25 +/-. (Figures based on an assortment of printer models with differing ink capacities per cartridge. Some pre-filled cartridge costs may be higher or lower. This is only an approximation).

Here's a photo of one of my bulk units to help you see how one of these little guys looks. Once you've got one set up and running smoothly, you'll love it!

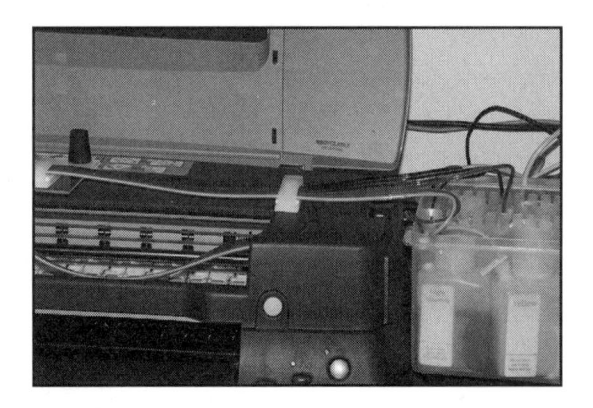

Q & A

Questions answered and instructions too!

Now it's time to answer some of the most commonly asked questions. Remember this isn't intended to replace the rest of the book, but will be a great reference for some of the problems you may run into.

Q. How will I know if the inks I use are going to fade or bleed when they're washed?

A. There are a couple of things to do. First of all, you want to buy a set of good pigmented inks. If you are using a dye-based ink, you will probably have some bleeding and/or fading. This is explained in more detail in the Inks section of the "Setting up your Equipment" chapter. Even some pigmented inks could cause problems because some are made with dyes in them as well. To be sure that your inks will stand up to anything your customers can dish out, it is always a good idea to put them through a two-step testing process.

The first thing to do is to print two identical items (or print one and cut in half). You will wash one and the second one will be your comparison item. As you wash the first piece, you should compare it to the unwashed article to see how well it holds up.

Step one is the soak test. After you press your transfer using the ink and paper combination of your choice, you will want to run it under cold to warm water until it's completely soaked. Do not soak it in a sink or tub of water, though; just get it good and wet. This is to deter-

C1 » Questions & Answers – Instructions too!

mine whether your inks are going to bleed when a customer puts your product in the wash. If you soak it in a tub or sink, the dyes could bleed but the inks might dissipate in the water and you wouldn't be able to see it.

After your test item is completely soaked (do not wring it out), set it aside for approximately an hour. I use an empty bathtub so it won't drain onto anything and damage it. Make sure when you set it aside that you fold it so that the transfer area is resting on a non-transferred area. This way, if the inks are going to bleed, they'll bleed onto the white part of the shirt where you can see them.

While your customers may not always put your products through a "worst case scenario," you want to know what would happen if they do. So, don't go easy on your test pieces; give 'em the worst you can dish out.

There are several people in this industry who sell their products in tourist areas where customers might buy a shirt and then either sweat, swim, or play around and get it wet before it's washed the first time. It is especially important for businesses with this type of customers to get the best quality ink and paper combination possible.

I've heard stories of customers buying a shirt, jumping into a boat or pool and coming back later to complain that the ink (usually black) bled all over the design. This can be avoided by using a good pigmented ink that has been proven by passing these tests.

The second step is the wash test. Simply wash and dry the test item as you would any other article of clothing. Do not take it out immediately; let it sit in the washer about an hour or so after the wash cycle has completed (another chance to notice whether it might bleed).

If you haven't seen any bleeding during these tests, your inks should be safe enough to satisfy the toughest customers. Just to be safe, continue to wash/dry, wash/dry, your test item. You should wash/dry it at least ten times.

Then, remember to compare the washed item to the unwashed item to see how much (if any) noticeable fading has occurred. Your goal is for there to be only very slight fading or none at all.

Q. I really messed up! I put the heat press down onto the printed side of my transfer and now I have gunk all over the hot part. What do I do now?

A. This has happened to me and just about every one in the industry as well I think. It's not such a big deal so don't panic. All presses are different. Some have a Teflon coating while others don't. If yours does, just let it cool down and wipe the mess away. Then clean any residue off after the press has totally cooled down.

If your press doesn't have a protective coating, the process might be a little more difficult but it should still come clean. Take a plastic spatula and, while the press is still hot, quickly scrape the melted transfer off. This should get rid of most of the mess. The remaining gunk can be wiped off with a towel. You'll probably never completely get rid of every trace but it should be fine once you reach the point where you can wipe it with a white towel and the towel stays white. I found that using a baby wipe works quite well and is mild enough that it won't damage anything.

C1 » Questions & Answers – Instructions too!

Q. I have an Epson brand printer already and found that it is compatible with a reputable 3rd party pigmented ink. Is there a special process to change over to the new inks?

A. This is very simple process. If you have ever changed ink cartridges in a printer, you'll find this process almost identical.

Make sure that any time you remove cartridges from your printer and then put them back in that you do it as quickly as possible. You don't want to give the printer time to dry out inside. If you're going to have open cartridges outside of the printer for more than a couple of minutes, you might also want to put them into a zipper bag to help keep them from drying out.

1. **Remove** previous cartridges by using the utility function in the Epson printing preferences windows. This will move the cartridges to a position that you can easily remove the old cartridges while also telling the printer that you are about to put new cartridges in. This is very important for the new cartridges to work successfully!

2. **Put** the removed cartridges aside (or in bag) or throw them away if you are certain you will never need them again. I'd recommend saving them, just in case. If you have a chipped printer, you definitely will want to save the cartridges. Even if you never use them again, some day you may need the chips that are on the outside of the cartridges.

3. **Now is the time** you will use the purging cartridges if you are going to. If not, it is time to either insert the cartridges or install the bulk unit. When you're finished with the installation, you should print at least six pages

of color bars which will hopefully eliminate the remaining inks that are in the printer. Some people don't use the purging cartridges and have no problem but I wouldn't want to take that chance.

3. **Gently remove** the yellow tape on each cartridge (preferably over a sink or some rags, in case of a spill). Insert the cartridges into the printer immediately after removing the tape. Be careful; the yellow tape covers a vent hole. These vent holes go to the ink reservoir. If you see any trace of ink under the yellow tape before peeling, you should exercise extra caution. Removing the yellow tape breaks the seal and allows air to pass into the cartridge. Normally this will not spray inks, but use caution just in case.

4. **Insert cartridges** into the printer. Make sure they are inserted completely. It is especially important with chipped printers to firmly, but carefully insert the cartridges into the proper areas. Inserting a cartridge when the chip is not inserted, or is not properly inserted into the cartridge will cause permanent fatal damage to your printer (just ask my 1280).

5. **Hit the button** on the printer that tells it to move the carriage over. Wait for it to charge the cartridges. Skipping this step could cause many minutes (or hours) of headache trying to figure out why it isn't printing well.

6. **Run a print head cleaning** cycle and then a print test page (in your printer utility menu) to see how many of the bars appear on the test page. It is very likely that some, but not all will show up at this point. I recommend printing 2 pages of bars (not the ones in the utility section, but here... 4 color or 6 color) at a DPI setting of at least 720, possibly 1440.

C1 » Questions & Answers – Instructions too!

7. **From this point**, I recommend that if you are not getting good print quality, that you wait a minimum of 15 minutes between each function. This is for several reasons but primarily because time is a friend to ink problems. Sometimes the air inside the cartridge has not yet had time to stabilize, sometimes there might be air pockets inside the cartridge from traveling or jostling.

It is not uncommon to require 2-3 print head cleanings followed by a test print page (again, about 15 minutes apart to reduce waste of ink). You might need to increase the DPI to the highest possible setting temporarily. Once you get a nice print, try reducing the DPI to 720 again. This isn't always possible on the C80 or C82 printers as they seem to always require the highest DPI.

Q. I think I'd like to get a Dye Sub setup as a second system. That would be a printer, inks, color profile and paper. Would I need anything else? I have a batch of mugs and some mug wraps.

A. That sounds about right. You might also want to consider buying a sheet of Teflon to protect the heat press as well as to buffer the heat for certain fabrics. Make sure that the printer you choose is compatible with the dye sub inks that you plan to purchase. You might also consider purchasing a bulk ink supply unit. I highly recommend them as they can greatly reduce your cost per print, reduce refilling headaches and reduce the costs of disposable prefilled cartridges.

Q. I want to do 2-sided shirts... Is this possible, and how do I go about it?

A. Yes, it's definitely possible! It's actually very simple too. Basically, you just want to have something handy to protect the bottom pad (Teflon sheet-recommended, smooth cardboard or even a sheet of paper will probably work).

For example, if you are going to press a pocket area graphic on the front and a larger back print, you would place the blank shirt on the press, and pre-press the shirt without a transfer for a recommended 3-6 seconds.

Based on my paper instructions, place the first transfer, press for 10-12 seconds at the temperature you typically use. Peel immediately.

Then, flip the shirt and place it on top of the Teflon sheet (so the first side is touching the Teflon, thus protecting the platen from the fresh transfer); no need for another pre-press.

Put the second transfer in place and press for 10-12 seconds as you did the first one. Peel immediately.

The only difference is that you peel the first one immediately. Do not keep the paper backing on it. And use the Teflon to protect the transfer and the heat platen when doing the second side. Voila!

Q. I keep hearing that I need to use medium to heavy pressure. I see this knob on my press but don't know how to adjust it or how I'd even know if the pressure is medium or heavy. Do I need to change the knob all the time?

A. No, and to be honest with you, I have even seen places where they call for a specific amount of pressure, for example, 60#. I have yet to see a press that specifically tells you what the rated pressure is.

C1 » Questions & Answers – Instructions too!

I do adjust the pressure on my press to compensate for the thickness of different items. For instance, on a sweatshirt, I have to raise the heat platen up to allow more room for the thicker material. When I am doing a baby bib or similar thin material, I adjust the heat platen down so that it will still have a good amount of pressure.

I wish I could give a 100% definite answer to this. My basic rule of thumb is that it should be mildly difficult to close into a locking position. If it doesn't have a noticeable lock down pressure, twist the knob to lower the heat plate closer toward the bottom platen.

On the other hand, if it's very difficult to close and lock, you could damage your press by forcing it to lock down. Remember it's not a suitcase and forcing it isn't going to have positive results. There is a middle ground that I am sure you'll find quickly.

Q. I just tried printing a design with red in it and it looks pinkish. Is there something special I should use or am I running out of some color the printer needs to make red?

A. That's actually a common problem. I'm not sure if it's an Epson printer issue or a 3rd party ink issue, but it seems to happen to many people, regardless of the inks they use. What is happening probably isn't that you're running out of ink already. Most likely your printer is just not printing all the colors properly.

The simple way to check is to go to the Printer Preferences section on your printer icon. Click on the Utility or Maintenance tab and then click on the Nozzle Check icon. You should print the very brief page of mini grids/bars. You will notice that you are likely not printing all of the black bars or some other color if another color is not printing correctly.

Just do a Print Head Cleaning from that same area in your printer utility. Then print another Nozzle Check to see if it is better. The next step would be to increase your DPI setting to a higher DPI. I leave mine between 720 and 1440 depending on the printer.

Never do more than 3 print head cleanings in a row because doing multiple print head cleanings will eventually burn out the print head(s). If you do a head cleaning, print a nozzle check page and if it still isn't good enough, wait about 15 minutes before trying again. If you do this 3 times and still don't get good results, it might just be that you are actually out of ink(s).

Q. Do I need a special cleaner for my press?

A. Most likely you will not. I wipe my press while hot with a blank mousepad daily. In addition to that, if I press a colored blank, I will wipe it down again to help prevent any shadowing effect on the next blank.

If you don't see your particular question here, don't worry. Just get online and look up the **I Made That!** forum. You're welcome to ask questions in this forum whenever they come up. I monitor the forum daily and will try to help you find answers.

Remember access is free for anyone who purchased this book, so use it often. Hope to see you there!

http://press2success.com/imadethat/

C2 » Stay Up To Date on the Internet

Stay Up to Date on the Internet

This is a brief listing of online forums for you to get some interaction with other people in the trade. Many forums are geared toward other systems than what we're using which can be confusing or overwhelming at first.

I recommend that you join one or two at first. As you become more familiar with the different processes, you'll be able to digest the information more easily, which should help you get up and running faster.

Forums

Support Forum for I Made That!
The most up to date information on suppliers, forums, and help getting your heat transfer business set up.

http://press2success.com/imadethat/

General Transfer Forum

http://groups.yahoo.com/group/Heat_Transfers_For_Desktop_Printers/

Screen Printing

http://www.screenprinters.net/

Dye Sublimation

http://www.dyesub.org/

Vendor Directory

The list below is far from complete. There are very likely hundreds of places to buy equipment and supplies. For additional resources, please feel free visit the Vendors section of our online forum.

http://press2success/imadethat/

Bulk Ink Units
http://www.easyflowsystems.com
http://www.inksupply.com
http://www.inkjetart.com

Button Making and ID Badge Supplies
Badge-A-Minit- http://www.badgeaminit.com
CompID - http://www.compid.com/
TLM Supply House - http://personalizedsupplies.com/

General Supplies- Paper, Inks, Presses, etc.
QLT- http://www.qlt.com
RPL Supplies - http://www.rplsupplies.com
TLM Supply House - http://personalizedsupplies.com

Heat Tape
http://personalizedsupplies.com

T-Shirts and Apparel, Tote Bags, etc.
Broder Brothers- http://www.broderbros.com/
Staton Wholesale- http://www.statonwholesale.com/
Virginia Tees - http://www.virginiats.com/

Stock, Preprinted Screenprinted Transfers
Impulse Wear - http://www.impulsewear.com/
Transfer Express - http://www.txpress.com/

Resources

Here you will find several Web sites and book titles that offer additional information, locations, or other potentially helpful data. Hopefully these will help give you some more background, hard-to-find information, business basics, and fresh ideas. Happy Hunting!

Online Resources

Flea Markets

http://collectors.org/FM/

http://www.keysfleamarket.com/fleamarket/

http://fleamarket.directoryusa.biz/

Business Help Groups

http://www.score.org/

http://www.sba.gov/

Business Plan Help

http://www.sba.gov/starting_business/planning/basic.html

http://www.bplans.com/

http://www.planware.org/freeware.htm

http://www.myownbusiness.org/

http://www.bulletproofbizplans.com/bpsample/Sample_Plan/sample_plan.html

More Online Resources

Craft/Arts

http://www.artscraftsshowbusiness.com/

http://www.craftsfaironline.com/Listings.html

http://www.craftsfairguide.com/

Fonts & Clip Art

http://www.1001freefonts.com/ultimatedownload.htm

http://www.thefreesite.com/Free_Fonts/

http://www.arttoday.com/

http://myfonts.com/WhatTheFont/

http://www.myfonts.com/

http://royaltyfreeclipart.com/

Online Auctions

http://www.ebay.com/

http://www.ubid.com/

http://www.onsale.com/

http://auctions.yahoo.com/

http://www.livedeal.com/

Books

The Public Domain: How to Find and Use Copyright-Free Writings, Music, Art & More by Stephen Fishman

The Complete E-Commerce Book:Design, Build & Maintain a Successful Web-based Business by Janice Reynolds, Roya Mofazali

Selling Online: How to Become a Successful E-Commerce Merchant by Jim Carroll, Rick Broadhead

Starting an Online Business For Dummies by Greg Holden

The Official eBay Guide to Buying, Selling, and Collecting Just About Anything by Laura Fisher Kaiser, Michael B. Kaiser, Pierre Omidyar

The Official Directory to U.S. Flea Markets by Kitty Werner

U.S. Flea Market Directory (Confident Collector Series) by Albert Lafarge

The Crafts Business Answer Book & Resource Guide: Answers to Hundreds of Troublesome Questions About Starting, Marketing, and Managing a Homebased Business Efficiently, Legally, and Profitably by Barbara Brabec

Purple Cow – Transform Your Business By Being Remarkable by Seth Godin

C4» Resources

Sample Frequent Buyer Card (Corel & Tiff format)

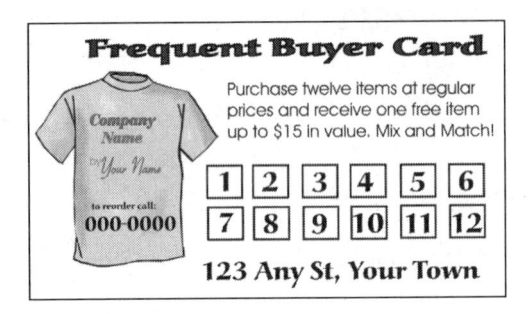

Sample Invoice Template (Word format)

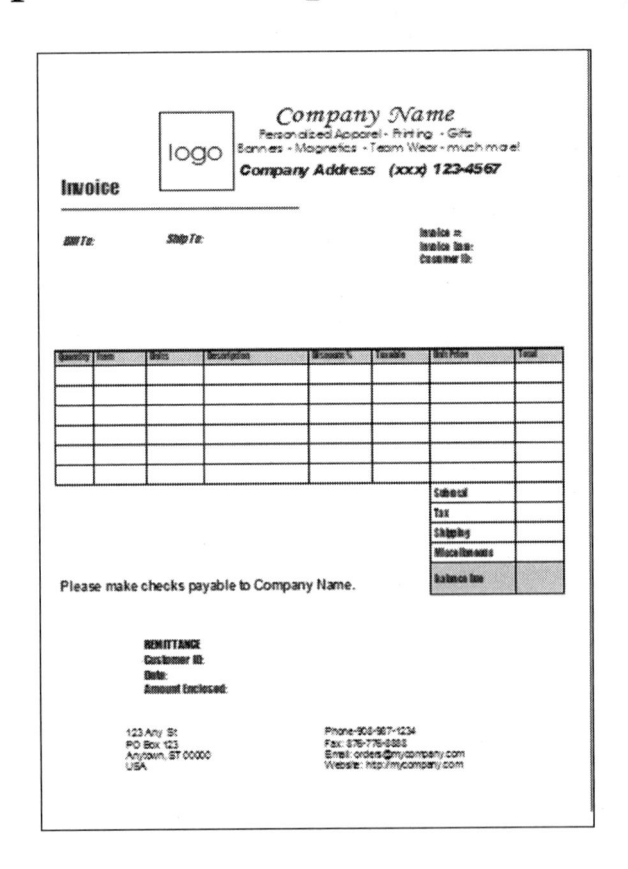

Companion CD

Remember your companion CD! Several goodies are included that will help you get the most from this book. On the CD, you'll find:

Color Version E-Book

Support Site URLs

Supplier URLs

Photo Section of Assorted Products

Templates for Creating:

Work Orders

Frequent Buyer Cards

Ads

And much more!

C4 » Resources

Sample Work Order Template (Corel Format)

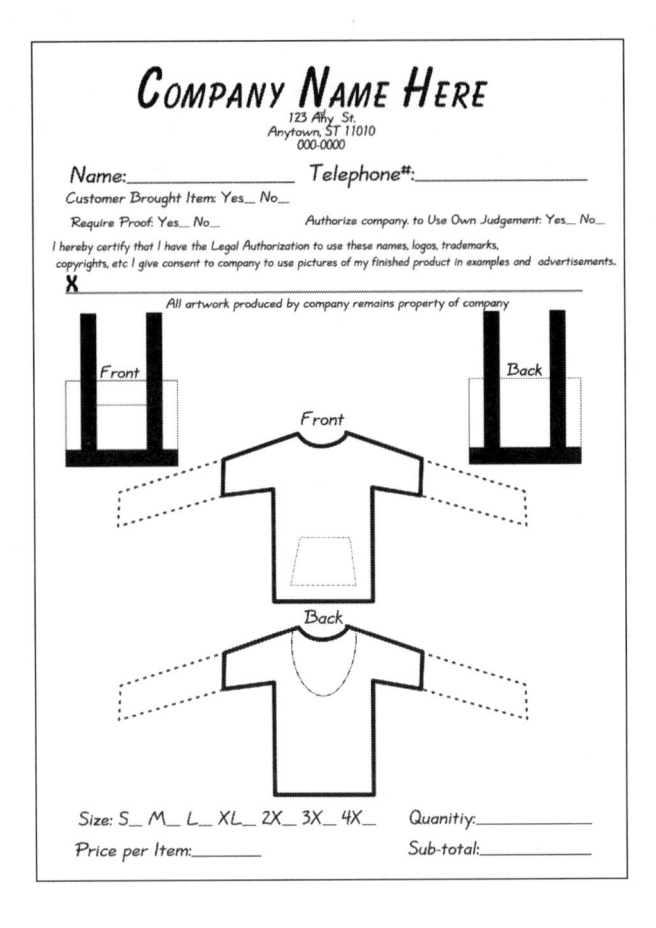

Glossary

Align: The process of aligning your blank imprintable or transfer on a surface so that they will be straight and centered on the final product.

All In One: This is a term given for a piece of equipment that performs more than one function. For our use, these units should do scanning, printing, and copying. Other brands also might include telephone and fax capabilities.

Application Tape: Very much like it sounds, application tape is used by adhering to a vinyl. Depending on the vinyl type and project you are making, it is typically then placed and adhered to a blank imprintable. See Signs chapter.

Archival Ink: These permanent inks are expected to last for years. In truth, both Pigmented Inks and Dye Sublimation Inks could be considered Archival Inks based on the fact that both, when done properly, will last for an extended period of time. However, normally when people use the term Archival Inks, they are referring specifically to Pigmented Inks.

Baby Wipes: Granted, probably not what you would expect to see in a glossary of personalized product items. I found out completely by accident (and the fact that I had an infant) that baby wipes can become one of your best friends when dealing with inks and areas that need to be kept clean and lint free. No need for expensive ones, nor would I recommend the ones with detergents in them, but it's definitely a good idea to keep some baby wipes around.

Blank: A blank is short for Blank Imprintable. These could be any item or any substrate that you will press your transfer onto. Most often, blanks are unprinted t-shirts, mouse pads, puzzles, and so on.

Bulk Unit: Also called a CIS or Continuous Ink System, a bulk unit is a collection of ink cartridges, thin hoses, and bulk ink bottles that delivers a continuous flow of ink to the printer. Not only will this save you the time and trouble of refilling your ink carts but it will save you a lot of money over refilling your own cartridges and even more money over buying prefilled carts. There is one bottle of ink for each color. There are several different manufacturers for bulk units. You should ask for referrals from others who use them to avoid purchasing a system that is poorly assembled or difficult to install.

Business Plan: A plan, usually written or typed on paper, which outlines the plan of action from business startup to fruition including goals, marketing, and financial issues.

Button Press: A smaller press that creates buttons in assorted sizes. Prices range from $40 to $1000+ depending on whether you want a manual or automatic press and other variables.

Cartridge Capacity: The amount of ink that a cartridge is intended to hold. These can sometimes hold more or less than the capacity amount. Cartridges now come with chips that tell the printer to stop printing when the chip believes that the cartridge is empty. Putting too much ink into a cartridge would result in wasted ink. You can view a chart of ink cartridge capacities at http://personalizedsupplies.com/cartridgecapacitylist.htm.

Chip Resetter: An electronic device created by techies to reset/reprogram the OEM (Original Equipment

Manufacturer) Epson chips that are on the outside of most newer models of Epson brand printer cartridges. The resetters will not work on some 3rd party chips. To work with refillers, you will likely need to do a chip swap.

CLC: Color Laser Copier

CLP: Color Laser Printer

Clamshell: A type of heat press. The word clamshell refers to the way the top heat plate pulls down onto the bottom platen at an angle, like a clam shutting. The other type is a Swing Away.

Cool Peel: As it sounds, this is a method of peeling the transfer paper away from a freshly pressed blank imprintable after it has had several seconds to cool down. Please note that cool peel is not typically the same as a cold peel. If you allow it to cool too much, you might run into problems. Sometimes cool peel and cold peel terms are used interchangeably, but I would recommend reading the instructions carefully to reduce risk of ruined projects.

Dedicated Printer: A dedicated printer is one which is used specifically for one purpose only. Many people who print their transfers using a pigmented ink will also be able to use that same printer and inks for their every day printing as well. When a person uses the dye sublimation method however, it is highly advisable that they use a dedicated printer to reduce unnecessary ink use and hold down the expense of these inks.

Dye Sublimation: A form of heat transfer. The inks are heated to the point where they become a gaseous form. The gas then impregnates the blank item and the ink becomes a permanent part of the blank. This method does not work with cotton material. Polyester material is the

C5 » Glossary

most commonly used for dye sublimation. This method is also used to decorate hard surfaces such as tiles, plates, mugs, etc. Pigmented ink transfers will not work on these products.

Eyeballing: Slang term used to describe a method of making measurements without tools. Visually aligning.

FPR: Fiberglass reinforced plastic. A commonly used material for use with dye sublimation.

Glass Etching: A method of personalizing glass products. There are different methods of personalizing onto glass including chemical and abrasive etching.

Graphics Program: A graphics program is a software application that allows you to do such things as create, edit and print graphic designs.

Hand: When you create a transfer it very often has a slightly stiff feel to it. This is called the hand. Most quality papers will become much softer after the first wash. If you use a paper that feels thick even after a wash or two, you might want to consider trying other transfer papers.

Heat Tape: A special tape that is often used in this industry to hold transfers in place. People who do dye sublimation transfers have a greater need for heat tape but it can also come in quite handy for standard transfer creation as well.

Heat Transfer: The process of moving a graphic from a printed paper to a blank item such as a t-shirt, mousepad, puzzle, towel, coaster, etc.

Hot Peel: Like it sounds, this is a method of peeling the transfer paper away from the freshly pressed blank imprintable immediately upon opening the heat press. If A hot peel is recommended, be sure to peel right away as it will begin to stick or cause other problems if you allow the transfer to cool.

ICC Color Profile: These are commonly associated with Dye Sublimation printing. Since the inks are not the same colors as the OEM Epson inks, these profiles are used by the computer to tell the printer how to get correct color. Color profiles are necessary for most brands of Dye Sublimation inks. They are not necessary with most Pigmented Inks (unless you're using an ink set that is not designed for Epson printers).

Landscape: This term describes the positioning of artwork or paper that is wider than it is tall.

Magic Mix: Magic Mix is a brand name for a line of pigmented archival inks. A line found to provide a superior heat transfer product that will not fade or bleed like many OEM inks and even some pigmented brands do.

Mirror Image: The act of flipping an artwork or printing a piece of artwork in a mirror, or backward/reverse mode. This is typically done on transfers. You print in mirror image, flip the transfer onto your blank imprintable, and when you peel away the transfer paper, your image is now in correct mode.

OEM Inks: Any ink that the Original Equipment Manufacturer created to be used with a specific product. Many printer companies do not warrant their equipment if damage to their equipment was caused by a third party product. This does not void the warranty for failure of the product for other reasons however, only if the damage was caused by the third party product.

Opaque Transfer: This method is commonly used for

C5 » Glossary

digital artwork that needs to be placed onto dark materials. Be aware that the projected life expectancy of an opaque transfer is typically much shorter than that of a regular transfer. It also often has a much heavier hand. A more long-term option for putting line art and text onto dark blanks would be thermal vinyl. For digital artwork, this is the best option although you will be limited to flat colors with vinyl while opaque transfers allow you to print your full spectrum of colors.

Orientation: This term is used when deciding if you want to create, edit, or print a graphic or artwork in landscape or portrait mode.

Pigmented Ink Transfers: This method is most commonly used in the personalized apparel business. Not to be confused with "hobby" transfers printed with OEM inks and applied with a household iron, pigmented ink transfers can be used to create professional quality products such as t-shirts, mousepads, puzzles, coasters, and more. Other (amateur) products can bleed and/or fade if they become wet or are thrown in the wash.

Portrait: This term describes the positioning of artwork or paper that is taller than it is wide.

Pre-Press: You should always pre-press your blank before applying and pressing the transfer. Quite often blanks will contain humidity or chemicals from manufacturing and the pre-press helps to force them out. To pre-press, just lower the press onto the blank for 3-6 seconds before opening the press placing your transfer to do the 'real' press.

Pressure: When you drop the press arm to begin the transfer, there are a few very basic pressure settings to consider. Light, Medium, and Heavy. I find that for most of my transfers I use medium to heavy pressure. You will want to adjust this setting based on the thickness of your blank imprintable.

Prime: Priming is a necessary step in preparing a cartridge to print. Often, an OEM cartridge will come already primed. However, with many refilling cartridges, it is necessary to prime the cartridges. In most (if not all) of the newer models, this is also called charging. If you install your cartridge into the printer and use the utility/maintenance function to do it, your cartridges will automatically go through a charging process which then allows you to begin printing almost immediately.

Print Head Cleaning: This is a maintenance or utility function that is performed when a print nozzle check is not printing adequately. It helps to clean the print head(s) that are not printing well. For more information on print head cleaning, see the Scanners & Printers chapter as well as the owner manual for your particular printer.

Print Nozzle Check: This is a maintenance or utility function that is performed on a printer to make sure that it is printing all of the colors properly. See the Scanners & Printers chapter.

Purge: Purging is a maintenance or repair action that is often performed when switching from one ink type to a different type. It clears the printer of the previous ink, leaving it ready for the new ink. It is done to prevent clogging of the print head and will also help to keep your new ink from being contaminated by what was left behind from the old ink. It can also be used to help clean the printer once it has become clogged.

C5 » Glossary

Royalty Free: Royalty free is a term used for graphics and/or artwork that does not require a royalty fee each time the art is used. Royalty free artwork is typically purchased once and can then be used as often as the buyer likes. Be very careful to read the license agreement for any graphics or artwork that you purchase. They are not all the same. Some licenses only permit personal use, and do not allow the art to be used for any items that will be sold!

Scanner: A piece of equipment used to electronically transfer a hard copy of a photo or other flat object to a computer file. This is often used in our industry to copy a photograph to print and transfer it onto an assortment of blank imprintables.

Screen Print: The process of using screens and inks much thicker than normal printer ink to adhere inks directly to blank imprintables. An alternative to this can also be to screen print to a special transfer paper. This is how commercial / stock transfers are created. They are sold to other businesses who then press them onto shirts on demand. Screen printing can be less expensive for large runs but will be considerably more for just a few shirts.

Set: Setting is a process that typically involves rubbing over a freshly transferred material (usually a thermal vinyl or opaque paper). The rubbing helps ensure that the transfer is fully adhered to the blank. You can use a towel or pot holder (or anything heat resistant to protect your hands from the heat). I use a blank mousepad when I set a transfer. If it doesn't set properly, you may need to re-press the item.

Soak Test: A test that is performed to see if the ink and paper combination that you are using will bleed or fade for your customers. See Q & A, question one.

Swing Away: This is a type of heat press. Unlike clamshell presses, the swing away style allows the top plate of the press to stay horizontally level. The swing away press can swing out of the work area, then back over the garment when it's time to press. For items such as tiles, or other breakables, a swing away is recommended (though not required).

Teflon Sheet: Teflon sheets are used to protect surfaces from excessive heat. Some people use a sheet to cover the bottom of the press. This type of teflon sheet can have an elastic edge around it so that it fits snugly around the bottom surface of the press. More often Teflon sheets are cut into specific sizes (usually same or slightly larger than the size of the press is ideal) and are available in varying thicknesses. They are often used when pressing two-sided blanks such as front/back of a shirt. Teflon can also be used when pressing an item where the blank is smaller than the transfer paper. The overhang of the paper/transfer will melt over onto the Teflon rather than damaging the press. Teflon sheets are often use with dye sub printing while they are more of an optional item with pigmented ink transfers.

Thermal Vinyl: A material used with a plotter and heat press to create a vector art text and/or graphic that can be heat applied to a large variety of materials. See Thermal Vinyl tutorial.

Third Party Inks: This term is frequently used when discussing any ink from a vendor or manufacturer other than the OEM. You might be inclined to associate inferior quality with third party inks but this is far from the reality. Sure, there probably are some inferior third party inks in production but there are also some that will give you far

C5 » Glossary

better results than those that come with your printer. Remember not to let one (or more) bad apple spoil your opinion of third party inks.

Thumper: Slang for a padded object that I keep around to 'thump' a cartridge against when filling/refilling cartridges. I purchased a wrist rest at a local office supply store, cut it into pieces, and now have three thumpers.

Transfer Paper: This is a special type of paper that is used to receive inks for the purpose of transferring the ink to another medium such as a shirt or tile or mousepad. While this book deals primarily with inkjet transfers, there are other types of transfer papers that are made for use with laser printers and other types of printers. Be sure you purchase the correct transfer paper for your printer whether laser, inkjet or other.

Vacuum: No, we're not talking about cleaning house here. We are talking about cleaning air out of a new cartridge. Creating a vacuum in a cartridge is typically only done with new, unused cartridges. It is frequently performed when setting up a bulk ink unit. See the "Refilling, Is it For You?" section.

Wash Test: This is a test performed to see if your paper and ink combination will fade or bleed over time. See Q & A, question one.

Weed: Weeding is the process of pulling away the undesired portion of a vinyl material. Whether you are making signs or thermal vinyl transfers, the process of pulling away the unwanted vinyl is necessary. Some might use special tools to do this. I have found that a needle from a ink refill kit or a simple push pin style thumb tack works very well for me.

Index

Align, 100-110, 175

All In One, 175

Application Tape, 142-144, 175

Archival Ink, 34, 53-54, 175

Baby Wipes, 148, 150, 175

Blank, 168, 176

Bulk Unit, 156, 176

Business Plan, 19-31, 176

Button Press, 67-68

Cartridge Capacity, 152, 176

Chip Resetter, 150, 177

CLC, 177

CLP, 177

Clamshell, 177

Cool Peel, 177

DDI & DPI, 82-85

Dedicated Printer, 177

Dye Sublimation, 45, 71-74, 177

Eyeballing, 100, 178

FPR, 178

Glass Etching, 69-70, 178

C6 » Index

Graphics Program, 33, 35-37, 178

Hand, 56, 178

Heat Tape, 178

Heat Transfer, 111-126

Hot Peel, 178-179

ICC Color Profile, 73-74, 179

Landscape, 90, 179

Magic Mix, 34, 179

Mirror Image, 90, 179

OEM Inks, 34, 52, 54-55, 179

Opaque Transfer, 123-126, 180

Portrait, 90, 180

Pre-Press, 114-115, 180

Pressure, 163-164, 180-181

Prime, 97, 181

Printer, 33-34, 49-51, 82-99

Print Head Cleaning, 94-95, 181

Print Nozzle Check, 92-94, 181

Printer Settings, 86-99

Purge, 96-97, 181

Scanner, 97-99, 182

Set, 130

Signs, 77-79

Soak Test, 157-159, 182

Teflon Sheet, 134, 183

Thermal Vinyl, 75-76, 127-131, 183

Third Party Inks, 34, 183-184

Thumper, 149, 184

Transfer Paper, 34, 56-58, 184

Vacuum, 146-147, 184

Wash Test, 157-159, 184

Weeding, 184

A Chat With the Author

Well, I hope this book has been a help to you. I hope that you have found at least one or two pieces of information that saved you more than the price of this book by helping you to avoid making costly mistakes.

Remember that there really aren't many things that can stand in the way of your becoming successful. Your biggest asset or barrier on your road to success is likely to be your own state of mind.

There are so many things that could go wrong in life and in business. What is important is that you keep a positive attitude as you learn and grow in your expertise with your new business.

There will likely be times that you are so down and depressed that you will probably consider putting everything up for sale. Your mind will begin to tell you that you would be better off waiting tables, or selling cars or whatever you did before you decided to start a business of your own.

I won't lie and say that you are guaranteed to succeed in this business, but I do feel confident enough to say that as long as you decide to stick with it, you can outlast the feelings of wanting to give up.

As with any business, it takes time to build your customer base. It takes time to learn to become the expert that you can become. It will be up to you to decide if you are willing to continue to invest your time and energy into your new business.

If you stick with it, you should always grab any chances you get to learn from those who are further along in their business, and you will learn from your own mistakes as well. I feel strongly that you will be successful. It's all about time and effort. If you refuse to stop giving putting forth your best effort, how can you not become successful?

If you plan to create products and sell them exclusively online, please make sure that you have realistic expectations for your Web-based business. This type of business will probably take more time than if you decide to market your business in more traditional ways, putting your products out in the customers view. But it can be done. Remember also what I said at the beginning of the book, *reevaluate often*.

If something isn't working, think it over. Figure out what isn't working. Always be aware of trends in the retail market. Don't copy others, but use your knowledge of the trends as a good way to come up with your own product ideas.

I love hearing about everyone's first transfer, the first paying job, the first big order, etc. If you have time, and don't mind sharing your successes with me and other members of my forum, please join us and share your successes and your failures. That way, we can all learn from each other's mistakes rather than having to make them all ourselves.

When you have questions and you can't find the answers in the book, be sure to visit the forum then as well. I will

C7 » A Chat With the Author

be monitoring it very often. I truly want to be able to help you if I can.

This book was written with the hope that it would be a resource tool for people who need a little bit of hand-holding while first getting their business set up and then along the way as you and your business grow together.

You may have realized by now that I am both an author and a supplier for this industry. While this might make a couple of people wonder if I wrote the book to simply boost sales for my supply company, I want to assure you that that's not my primary motivation.

When I was getting started, I fought for months after buying my first equipment setup (that I would have been better off without). I remember how difficult it was to have no one and no place to turn for help, and wondered why the vendors weren't more helpful. Sure, they were very nice and friendly, but none seemed interested in helping me learn.

When I decided to go into selling supplies for this industry I promised myself that I would be for my customers what I didn't find from the vendors that I originally patronized... a friend in the business.

So, I decided to put as much free information on my website as I could. I answer individual emails more hours a day than some people are awake. I do it because I love to help people.

Our supplies business fully supports my kids and myself and we count on our business to keep us together. God has richly blessed us and I have never had to take a job outside of the home since my son was born (I wish I could have said the same with my daughter).

I want you to know that I will not treat you any differently whether you buy your supplies from me or not. My goal is to help others become successful so that they can have a better life for their family and their own peace of mind. If I can do that, I will trust that my family will also be taken care of.

As I began to find it tougher and tougher to answer every email with a thorough and easy to understand answer, I realized it was time for me to write a book. This will allow me help more people with the basics. Then, when you are ready to get into the specifics, I can help you tailor your supplies and equipment shopping list to what will best suit your individual situation.

I really want to thank you for buying this book and supporting small business. I can't wait to get to know you better on the Internet forum when you are ready to stop in for a visit.

http://press2success.com/imadethat/

As you progress, and are ready to add additional heat transfer methods, I'll be glad to help with more online resources as well as additional forums where the groups specialize in the specific system that you're using.

There will likely come a time when you will stop and think back on your learning process. You will be sitting at the table with your family or a friend and, somewhere along the line, you will realize that **You Made It!**

What a terrific feeling. I wish you all the best! Now, don't forget to check out the I Made That! forum online.

I Made That! » The End